# SING ME TO
# HEAVEN

*the story of a marriage*

## MARGARET KIM PETERSON

**Brazos Press**
A Division of Baker Book House Co
Grand Rapids, Michigan 49516

Published by Brazos Press
A division of Baker Book House Company
P.O. Box 6287, Grand Rapids, MI 49516–6287
www.brazospress.com

"Sing Me to Heaven" is by Jane Griner (text) and Daniel E. Gawthrop (music). ©1991 by Dunstan House, P.O. Box 220, Stephans City, Virginia 22655; www.DunstanHouse.com. Used by permission.

"People" from ALL THAT SUNLIGHT ©1967; © renewed 1995 by Charlotte Zolotow. Reprinted by permission of S©ott Treimel NY.

Printed in the United States of America

Library of Congress Cataloging-in-Publication Data
Peterson, Margaret Kim, 1961-
    Sing me to heaven : the story of a marriage / Margaret Kim Peterson.
        p.      cm.
    ISBN 1-58743-047-9
    1. Kim, Hyung Goo, 1957–1995. 2. Peterson, Margaret Kim, 1961–  3. AIDS
(Disease)—Patients—United States—Biography. 4. AIDS (Disease)—Patients—
United States—Family relationships. I. Title
RC606.55.K54P48 2003
362.1′ 969792′ 0092—dc21                                    2003002603

# IN MEMORY OF HYUNG GOO KIM

*December 7, 1957–September 17, 1995*

In my heart's sequestered chambers
   lie truths stripped of poet's gloss.
Words alone are vain and vacant
   and my heart is mute.

In response to aching silence
   memory summons half-heard voices,
and my soul finds primal eloquence
   and wraps me in song.

If you would comfort me, sing me a lullaby.
If you would win my heart, sing me a love song.
If you would mourn me and bring me to God,
sing me a requiem, sing me to heaven.

From *Sing Me to Heaven*
words by Jane Griner
music by Daniel Gawthrop

# CONTENTS

**Land and Sea: The Old Country**   7
The Most Beautiful of Absolute Disasters   9
*January 9, 1990:* The Announcement   17
A Marginal Man   20
*March 17, 1990:* Starting AZT   29
School Daze   37
Learning to Dance   45
The Clinic   52
**Land and Sea: Ascending**   63
*October 8, 1992:* KS Diagnosis   64
**Land and Sea: Bodies in the Water**   71
Dreaming with Salvador Dali   73
*September 30, 1993:* Leaving Work   80
Sing Me to Heaven   87
*January 6, 1994:* CMV Diagnosis   96
*March 14, 1994:* PCP Diagnosis   101
**Land and Sea: Out of Contact**   107
Some People   108
The Rhetoric of AIDS   115
A Green and Dying Tree   126
*April 1, 1995:* Foscarnet   136
The Gardens   145
**Land and Sea: Diving**   154
*September 4, 1995:* Hospitalization   156
**Land and Sea: Above the Clouds**   167
*September 17, 1995:* Death   169

**Land and Sea: In Midair**    176
*September 20, 1995:* Funeral    177
**Land and Sea: At the Wheel**    186
*October 7, 1995:* Burial    188
**Land and Sea: Wasteland**    194
Reconaissance    195
**Land and Sea: Flood Stage**    203
Almost Noble    205
*May 13, 1996:* Final Exam    213
**Land and Sea: Descending**    218
**Land and Sea: Living on the Ocean**    220

**Acknowledgments**    224

## LAND AND SEA

# THE OLD COUNTRY

A few months after Hyung Goo died, I had a dream in which I was sitting at a table, engaged in earnest conversation with a man I did not know. We were debating the merits of retracing the outlines of the past. Should one, for example, revisit a place—a grove of trees, say—that was important in one's childhood?

"There's no point in doing such a thing," the man said. "It's not something most people would do, and they get over it."

I disagreed. He was right that most people don't or wouldn't do it, but not because it doesn't matter. They wouldn't do it because it matters too much. It would be felt too deeply; it would evoke the kind of strong feeling that most people are afraid of. Most of us, if we went back to that grove of trees that meant so much, and stood under them and looked up at the sky through their branches or had a picnic under them, we'd cry; and most people don't want to cry. But by doing so, we'd fix those trees in our memory so that we would never be without them, even if we never came back and saw them again.

In my dream, I startled even myself with the vehemence, the passion with which I made my case to this man, who looked at me and listened and appeared to take my point, but said nothing in reply.

Is memory worth the price of grief? To remember sorrow is to grieve again. Remembered joy is joy that is no more and for that reason is itself a source of sorrow. And yet, to remember and to grieve is to honor those joys and those sorrows. It is to refuse to relinquish them to the past, and instead to claim them for the present and carry them into the future.

Or so I seemed to be trying to persuade myself. Hyung Goo and I had been married for four years before he died of AIDS. Those four years had been intensely happy and intensely sad, and had transformed both of us in ways we could hardly have imagined. Now, in the aftermath of that life, I wanted to remember. And yet, I was overwhelmed by the sadness entailed in the very act of memory. Who were the "people" I spoke of in the dream, who didn't want to cry? They were me. I didn't want to cry; and yet I did, all the time. As I explained the importance of memory, and of grief, to the man in my dream, I explained it to my divided self.

Years later, the intensity of that grief has faded. I remember Hyung Goo's and my life together as if it were a place I used to live: a much-loved and much-missed place, to which I can never return. From my life in a new world, I remember the old country. An emigrant's memories of the old country sometimes take on a rosy glow that obscures the difficulties and pains of the place. My memories of the country of our marriage seem similarly to have softened with the passage of time. The harshness of the landscape has faded, and I am left with an impression of almost unbearable beauty. However did I bear it, living in a place that was so lovely?

# THE MOST BEAUTIFUL
# OF ABSOLUTE DISASTERS

Falling in love with Hyung Goo was the best and the worst thing that ever happened to me. I was twenty-eight, and just emerging from about twenty very homely and awkward years. I had finally started to date, and was making the depressing discovery that I couldn't seem to meet anyone I really liked. I would be sitting across the table from some perfectly unobjectionable young man, thinking, "Just take me home. Take me home, and don't call me again."

Then, a week or two before Thanksgiving of 1989, Hyung Goo asked me out. I was only dimly aware of his existence. We were both sporadic attenders of a young people's group at Park Street Church in Boston, and had had a few brief conversations over the years. I thought his line of work had something to do with computers. In an indication of my complete ignorance of all things Korean, I had once seen his name written down and had thought, "Hyung Goo Kim—what a funny name."

Hyung Goo invited me to a concert by the Lydian String Quartet, the quartet in residence at Brandeis University. This was a group that played a lot of new music, and the day before the concert, Hyung Goo discovered that the entire program was to consist of pieces written within the last twenty years. Not sure that this would be my idea of a good time, he called me and offered to make an alternate plan. I wasn't particularly daunted. I had majored in music in college and had listened to

9

a lot of new music then. I told him I would be happy to attend the concert as planned.

We went to a Thai restaurant for dinner, where I was surprised to learn that Hyung Goo did not work with computers; he was a molecular biologist. We went on to the concert. It was cacophonous. Apparently the facility for listening to new music that I had developed in college had completely evaporated in the intervening years. Hyung Goo listened with rapt attention. At the end of one particularly ear-splitting piece, he turned to me and said with perfect seriousness, "You know, at the end of a piece like this, I just wish I could hear it again right away."

He took me home, and I didn't give him a second thought. Not that I hadn't enjoyed the evening—in fact, I had had a lovely time. But I was due to graduate from seminary in six months, after which I was planning to move away to start a doctoral program. I had already made up my mind that any romantic developments in my life were going to take place after I had left Boston, and not before. It didn't even occur to me to wonder why I had had such a nice time, and whether I might like to see more of Hyung Goo. When, a few weeks later, Hyung Goo called and asked if I would like to go with a group of friends to a Messiah sing, I was happy to accept. It was, after all, a group event and thus not really a date. I reciprocated with an invitation to a Christmas party—again, a group event and thus not a date.

On New Year's Eve, Hyung Goo invited me to a formal party that one of our mutual friends gave every year as a benefit for the library of the school where she taught. Before the party, we had dinner at the home of some friends. The evening took an unexpected turn when our hostess cut her finger while preparing the meal. She bandaged it up, but after dinner it became apparent that more than a bandage was required. Hyung Goo volunteered to take her to the emergency room, and suggested I go on ahead to the party with everyone else. "No, no," I said. "I'll come to the emergency room with you."

When we arrived at the hospital, Cathy disappeared into the treatment area of the emergency room. Hyung Goo and I sat in the otherwise deserted waiting room, he in his tuxedo, me in my evening dress. There was nothing to do but talk, so we talked, for hours, about anything and everything: life, work, children, music. Years later that interlude came to seem a strange fore-shadowing of things to come: the two of us alone together, in a hospital, a space at once public and intensely private, waiting for we knew not how long, and in that seeming void reaping an unexpected harvest of companionship.

It was late in the evening before Cathy emerged from the bowels of the emergency room, an enormous bandage around her finger covering the several stitches that had been required to close the wound. "Get me out of here," she hissed. We assumed that she would want to go home to bed, but she was not about to have her entire evening ruined by a cut on the finger. We dropped by her house so she could change her clothes, and drove to the party. We arrived just a few minutes before mid-night to find the entire party abuzz with news of Cathy's acci-dent and relief that we were all finally there. As Cathy and I went to the cloakroom to leave our coats, she asked, "So, are you and Hyung Goo dating?"

Perhaps at this moment I realized that I hoped so. But for all our talking that evening, there had been no conversation on this subject. What was he thinking? "I don't know," I said.

Hyung Goo took me home from the party at about two in the morning. As we said goodnight, he gave me a kiss on the cheek, somewhere in the vicinity of my left ear. Interesting, I thought. The next day there was another party to attend; a few days later there was a concert. A few days after that I had a graduate-study-related interview during the day. Hyung Goo came by after his evening rehearsal with the Tanglewood Fes-tival Chorus, ostensibly to hear how my interview had gone. As he was about to leave, he said, "Can I talk to you about something?"

I could tell this was serious. I led him into the study, and we sat down. In the same quiet, measured tone that I had already come to love, Hyung Goo told me that he was infected with HIV, the virus that causes AIDS, and my entire world collapsed around me. I had never met anyone whom I liked half so much as I liked him. I had never met anyone who made me feel so

11

whole, who was such good company, whose interests paralleled and complemented mine the way his did. He was a musician, he was a scientist, he was a thoughtful and committed Christian. He was handsome, funny, considerate, creative. He owned a tuxedo, for goodness' sake. And he was going to die of AIDS. He didn't have just some tiny, negligible thing wrong with him. He didn't even have something big but manageable wrong with him. He had the single worst thing imaginable wrong with him. I had always assumed that if I could just meet someone I liked, then I would live happily ever after. Now I'd met someone I liked, and we were definitely not going to live happily ever after. I felt like I had been kicked in the gut by the biggest boot in the world. It was years before I could draw a deep breath again.

Why didn't I show Hyung Goo the door, right then? I spent a long time puzzling over this in later years. At the time, my utterly unreflective response was to reach out for him and to hold on as if to life itself. I had been so lonely, for so long. I wanted so desperately to know and be known, to love and be loved, and I had never met anyone with whom that seemed like the remotest possibility. I could sense that possibility already welling up around the two of us. To have said to him at that point, "I'm sorry; would you please go away" would have felt like cutting off my arm. I just couldn't do it.

The practical result of Hyung Goo's disclosure of his HIV status was to catapult us from the holiday round of parties and concerts and romantic speculation about does-he-like-me-as-much-as-I-like-him, to an arena where the major questions had to do with life and death and were we going to marry each other or not. We spent hours talking about everything, hours during which I could only fall more deeply in love with him. And the more I loved him, the more trapped I felt. I felt at the same time that I had to marry him, and that I couldn't possibly marry him. I couldn't marry him because he was going to die of AIDS. He might give it to me, and then I'd die of AIDS too. We couldn't have children. We could be impoverished by the cost of his medical care. It was just impossible. On the other hand, I was sure I would never meet anyone else who was so right for me. It was inconceivable that there could be anyone else who could love me as he did, and whom I could love as I loved him. I had to marry him.

Finally, I had had enough. I had been accepted to a doctoral program at Duke University. I decided that I was going to break up with Hyung Goo, move to North Carolina, and get on with my life. It didn't work out quite the way I planned. I did break up with him and move to North Carolina and start my doctoral program. As I settled down in my new life, I began to feel more settled emotionally, too. The frenzy of anxiety that I had been in ever since that January day when Hyung Goo told me about his HIV status began to subside, as I set up my apartment and bought my books and started attending my classes. I was supplementing my stipend by tutoring undergraduates in organic chemistry. One beautiful autumn day I was walking on campus near the chemistry building, and I thought, "You know, I will survive. Life is pretty good. In fact, the only thing that would make life better would be if Hyung Goo were here."

At that moment it began to be possible for me to think of marrying Hyung Goo. The breakup had been awful. I had cried rivers of tears. Hyung Goo had been devastated. But it got me out of that trap in which I felt both that I had to marry him and that I couldn't marry him. Breaking off the relationship and moving away gave me enough space to realize that I didn't have to marry him, but I could marry him if I chose to. Yes, he was going to die of AIDS. I didn't like that, but I couldn't change it. Did I want to survive him as his widow or as his ex-girlfriend? I called Hyung Goo and asked if he were willing to reopen the question.

Hyung Goo was astonished. He had told me he was going to hope that I would change my mind. Perhaps a cure for AIDS would be forthcoming and that would allow me to feel that I could marry him. I was thoroughly annoyed by his determination to hope I would change my mind. I didn't think there was going to be any cure for AIDS before he died of it, and in any case, I hadn't come lightly to the conclusion that I could not marry him. I was not going to change my mind. When within a matter of months I had changed my mind, I was chagrined, and Hyung Goo was amazed.

We arranged that I would spend a few weeks with him over the Christmas holidays, and we would make our decision then. We knew we wanted to marry one another, but we worried that AIDS might have so dominated our thinking that we might have failed to consider some other important issues. We bought a little handbook for couples considering marriage, and dutifully worked our way through it. At the end, we looked at one another and said, "Well, what's the decision?" We decided to get married, and the sooner the better. We knew we didn't have all the time in the world.

We were married about six months later, in June of 1991, at Park Street Church in Boston. We spent that summer house-sitting in Cambridge, and in late August returned to Durham so that I could begin my second year of doctoral studies. Hyung Goo got a job in a lab associated with Duke University Medical Center, and we began to settle into a kind of double life. We told virtually no one of Hyung Goo's HIV infection, and no one had any reason to suspect that anything was amiss. To all appearances, we were a nice young couple with all of the normal prospects and concerns of any young couple. I went to class; he went to work. We found a church, we made some friends, we attended concerts at Duke, we walked in the Duke gardens. That was our public life.

Then there was our life with AIDS. When we married, Hyung Goo had been taking AZT, the earliest drug developed to treat HIV infection itself, for over a year. When we moved to Durham, Hyung Goo became a patient at the Infectious Diseases Clinic at Duke. He had monthly appointments for the administration of a drug to prevent a certain kind of AIDS-related pneumonia. He met weekly for psychotherapy with the social worker who was his case manager. After a while, he began to develop various AIDS-related conditions, each requiring some new kind of medication. My anxiety grew to the point that I started seeing a psychotherapist as well. HIV and AIDS dominated our conscious concerns, but this aspect of our life was largely hidden from those around us.

There was another sense in which we lived a double life in those years. I am aware of this as I look back over our photograph albums and the letters that I wrote to friends who knew of Hyung Goo's HIV infection. The tone of the letters can only be described as apocalyptic. I was always expecting disaster to strike. At first these concerns were overblown—as I know now, no one with HIV infection becomes deathly ill overnight. But there was never a moment in which I wasn't aware that there was a little black cloud on the horizon, one that threatened any minute to become a big black cloud that would blot out our life together. As Hyung Goo became more ill, my fears became more realistic, until in the last months of his life the letters describe not anticipated disaster but real disaster, as we staggered along, reeling from blow after blow after blow, trying desperately just to survive from one day to the next.

However did we survive, I wonder. Then I look at the photograph albums, and I remember. I remember the radiance, the exuberance, the joy in living and in each other. There are the pictures of our honeymoon in Maine, with Hyung Goo in one antic pose after another, so happy to be married he just didn't know what to do. There are the pictures we took at the Duke gardens, of more kinds of flowers than we had known existed. There are pictures of friends and family at holiday celebrations, pictures of us singing and playing in concerts, pictures taken in museums from Boston to Chicago to Los Angeles. At the Field Museum in Chicago, we saw a silly exhibit about the space shuttle that included a film that required 3-D glasses for viewing. We kept the 3-D glasses, and took pictures all over the country of us and other people wearing them: my brother and sister-in-law at their wedding, Hyung Goo's sister and brother-in-law at their wedding, Hyung Goo and several of his classmates at his fifteenth college reunion, the two of us on the beach at Cape Cod and Block Island.

These photographs capture in miniature the fundamental reality of our life: we were more alive together than either of us had ever been apart from the other. In time, the first duality in our lives coalesced into a unity as we began to tell people of Hyung Goo's illness, and no longer tried to present to the world a public face that was somehow unconnected with AIDS. But the second duality only intensified as time went on. The longer we were married, the sicker Hyung Goo got, and the more intensely happy in one another we became. One of the social workers at the Infectious Diseases Clinic once said to us, "You know, there are a lot of people who wish they could find what the two of you have together." It was very odd to be at the same time the object of other people's envy and horror. We knew no one who would have wished to be in our shoes where Hyung Goo's illness was concerned; and yet people often seemed to respond to the two of us together with a kind of wistful longing.

Nevill Coghill, in the introduction to his translation of the *Canterbury Tales*, says that "all Chaucer's heroes regard love when it comes upon them as the most beautiful of absolute disasters, an agony as much desired as bemoaned." The love in question was not marital love, which, if it existed in the Middle Ages, was not the stuff of literature, but courtly love, the romance between a knight and a married lady who might or might not ever deign to drop her handkerchief in his direction. The idea of paying court to a woman who is married and therefore by definition unattainable has always seemed a little perverse to me. But perhaps part of the appeal of courtly love is rooted in a couple of fundamental truths: it is impossible in this life to love without grief; and, sometimes, where grief is intensified, love is intensified too. The medieval knight artificially intensified both grief and love by choosing as the object of his passion someone he could not possibly have. Our grief came in knowing, not that we could never have one another, but that we would certainly lose one another sooner rather than later. The brevity of our life together, the sorrows that accompanied it, the sweeping away of cherished illusions of "living happily ever after"—perhaps these were disasters. But it was a beautiful life, more beautiful than either of us could have imagined before we set out together.

# JANUARY 9, 1990: THE ANNOUNCEMENT

In 1990, AIDS had been an identifiable reality for about ten years. An HIV antibody test, making it possible to know whether an individual was infected with HIV, had been available for about five years. But HIV and AIDS were confined, for the most part, to certain at-risk populations, and I wasn't a member of any of them. I wasn't gay and male, or a drug user, or a prostitute. I wasn't a hemophiliac or a health-care worker. I wasn't socially located in any way that might have led me to think that AIDS was something with which I should concern myself. Along with many others, I thought of AIDS as something from another world, one I didn't live in.

Then Hyung Goo told me he was HIV-positive. I couldn't have been more stunned if he had set off a bomb in my living room. In the course of the several dates we had had to that point, he had told me that he had gone through a period of years in which he had questioned his "identity." It turned out that the identity he was talking about was, in part, his sexual identity, and the questioning had involved a great deal of sexual activity with both men and women. He had resolved the sexual-identity question by dint of extensive psychotherapy, but by then the damage was done: he had been infected with HIV.

Hyung Goo had learned of his HIV infection five years earlier, in 1985. The HIV-antibody test had recently become available to the general public, and he knew he was at risk, so he had himself tested. When the result came back positive, he received

17

it as a death sentence. He withdrew from virtually all relationship with anyone, and waited to die. A number of people he knew tested positive for HIV around the same time. Many of them did rapidly sicken and die, but Hyung Goo didn't. As a year, then two and three years, went by and Hyung Goo found himself still alive and otherwise healthy, he began to emerge from his death watch and reconnect with other people. He started a string quartet with friends from church; he joined the Tanglewood Festival Chorus.

And he began to hope again for significant relationship, for love, even for marriage. He had had a steady girlfriend at the time he tested positive for HIV. The relationship collapsed under the strain of that knowledge, and Hyung Goo found it difficult to imagine that anything other than a single life was a possibility for him. In the summer of 1989, that began to change. A couple of women in the chorus had expressed more than a friendly interest in him. Their interest had in each case evaporated when he had disclosed his HIV status, but he began to wonder whether perhaps, with the right person, there might be hope for the intimate relationship he longed for.

Hyung Goo approached this question in typically methodical fashion. Who among the women he knew might be a good candidate? Whom was he interested in getting to know better? Who might share enough of his interests to be able to get along with him? "Your name came to the top of the list," he told me later.

"Who else was on the list?" I asked.

But Hyung Goo was not only methodical; he was quick-thinking. "I never got beyond the first name," he said with a grin. Having made his one-name list, he proceeded to ask me out once, then several times; and then, on the evening of January 9, 1990, he told me of his HIV status.

I have two images of that January evening. One is of being struck by a speeding train. Was Hyung Goo at the controls of the train? Was he a passenger? Had he been hit by the same train? Perhaps all were true. Later, I realized I was angry. How could he have done this to me? How could he have pursued a relationship with me, when he knew his HIV status and I didn't? "I couldn't very well have said, 'Hi, I'm Hyung Goo Kim and I'm HIV-positive,'" he said. "I told you as soon as I was sure that interest was mutual." I knew this was the truth—but that didn't change the fact that for those first several weeks, when my heart was beginning to turn and open to his, like a plant turning to the sun, he had known and I hadn't. And in the wake of his announcement, I felt that I and all my hopes and expectations had been shattered on impact, with no hope that they or I would ever be the same again.

The other image of that evening is one of stillness, of a door swung open, of Hyung Goo waiting, gravely, to see whether I would turn away or step inside. He had opened that door on several other occasions. Every time, the person on the other side had turned away. There is a snapshot that was taken of the two of us ten days earlier, at the New Year's Eve party we attended. We're all dressed up, leaning toward one another, smiling for the camera. This picture hung on our bedroom wall, and for years, every time I looked at it, I would think, "That was before I knew." It seemed a picture of lost innocence, a picture of a very young person who knew nothing of the sorrows that lay just down the road. Then one day I looked at the picture, and thought, "That was before he knew, too." Hyung Goo, handsome, smiling, not knowing whether I would choose to step into his world once I knew what it was.

The door swung open, and I stepped in.

19

# A MARGINAL MAN

Hyung Goo was born in Korea in 1957 and immigrated to the United States in 1964, when he was seven years old. He lived the rest of his life in greater Boston and, after we were married, in North Carolina; but in certain respects he continued to encounter the world in ways that were very Korean. I was mystified when, in the early days of our marriage, I would set Hyung Goo's plate before him and he would look at it and say, "Hmm."

In desperation, I finally asked him, "What do you like?"

"I like everything!" he said, seemingly just as puzzled as I at why dinner never seemed to be to his taste.

Gradually, we figured it out. Hyung Goo did like everything, in the sense that he happily ate anything offered him in a restaurant or as a guest in someone's home. But our assumptions about what counted as normal food were completely different. I had a Western palate; he had an Asian one. To me, a normal dinner was meat and starch and a vegetable, and if I had extra time maybe I would gussy up one or more of the dishes with cream or cheese. To Hyung Goo, cream and cheese were foreign (and indigestible) ingredients, and any dish seasoned only with salt and pepper and herbs had "no flavor." To have flavor, a dish had to include red pepper, sesame oil, soy sauce, or garlic, singly or in combination. He didn't particularly care for bread, frustrating my efforts to feed him sandwiches for lunch. Finally I was enlightened by his social worker, who had lived for some years in Hong Kong. "He's Asian," she said. "If he's going to eat wheat, it has to be in the form of a noodle."

And he ate kimchee, Korean spicy fermented cabbage, with everything. I never learned to make this, and he would hunt through the refrigerated cases at our local Korean grocery for jars of kimchee that listed as an ingredient not just "fish paste" but anchovies. "There are many fish, but there is only one anchovy," he would say triumphantly, as he bore his prize to the cash register.

Eventually I began to see Hyung Goo's identity as a Korean-American not just as something that made him different from me, but in terms of his own experience as one who stood between cultures, and was fully at home nowhere. An annual event that underscored Hyung Goo's cultural homelessness was the New Year's Day gathering of his large extended family. Hyung Goo's parents were each one of eight children. His father's siblings were scattered all over the world, but all of his mother's siblings lived in suburban Boston or in New York City. On New Year's Day, all of the aunts and uncles and cousins on his mother's side would gather for a family celebration that included three principal ritual elements: a visit to Hyung Goo's grandfather's grave, a meal, and bowing.

The visit to the cemetery was unproblematic. The family stood in a circle around the grave while one of the uncles prayed at length in Korean, and then we all recited the Lord's Prayer together in English. The meal was wonderful. Hyung Goo was in his element as he downed great quantities of his aunts' cooking. But the bowing was a problem. All the relatives were dressed in their very best traditional Korean clothing: long brightly colored silk dresses for the women and girls, silk pants and jackets for the men and boys. The aunts and uncles, along with Hyung Goo's parents, would sit in a row on the couch (fortunately, it was a long couch). All the members of Hyung Goo's own generation formed a line, and bowed in turn to each of the aunts and uncles. This involved getting down on hands and knees, and touching the forehead to the floor. In return, each received an envelope filled with cash. As Hyung Goo's uncles were all hard-working and successful small-business owners, the amounts of money tended to be substantial.

For the members of Hyung Goo's parents' generation, this ceremony was an echo of the cultural patterns of authority and deference and patronage that they had grown up with. Hyung Goo's mother had bowed to her in-laws every day for the first year of her marriage. In a new country, where family relationships operated under much different rules, this once-a-year ritual served as reassurance that, on some level, the old patterns were still there. Children still respected their parents; the younger generation still deferred to the older; elders still were patrons of the young.

For the younger generation, the experience seemed to be more one of trick-or-treat. You bow, you get money. Of course they understood that there was an element of respect implied in bowing to parents and other elders. It was respect that they were happy to give, especially since compliance came with a monetary reward. But that was all it meant. It was something you do for your parents because it pleases them, and then you get money and have a big meal.

The difficulty for Hyung Goo was that he viewed bowing as a symbol of a patriarchal and authoritarian cultural system of which he wanted no part. Unlike his siblings and cousins, he could not see bowing as a simple gesture of respect. Unlike his aunts and uncles and parents, he could not see it as an expression of appropriate patterns of authority. He was caught between cultures: Korean enough to understand what bowing meant, but American enough not to like it. Alone among his siblings and cousins, he refused to bow.

Hyung Goo's parents were more or less resigned to this. They knew how utterly intransigent Hyung Goo was when he made up his mind. For a time, Hyung Goo's mother entertained hopes that she could get me to bow—after all, she had gotten her other white American daughters-in-law to bow. But then, her other sons were happy to bow themselves. I wasn't about to bow—I knew that to do so would be to choose my in-laws over Hyung Goo. At the same time, I didn't want open confrontation. When I saw people getting ready to bow, I would fade away, finding somewhere—anywhere—else to be for the short time the ritual took, and then fading back in as the cousins counted their money and everyone began to help themselves to food.

Even Hyung Goo's experience of language set him apart from both his native and his adopted cultures. He had emigrated from Korea speaking only Korean. He learned English in school, and while still a child formed a resolve to speak English perfectly. Perhaps as a result of this conscious intention, his English was a little too perfect. His older and younger brothers, both of whom had immigrated with him, spoke English as if they had been born in Boston, but Hyung Goo's English was always a little over-precise.

For their part, Hyung Goo's parents encouraged their children to speak English at home, as a result of which they forgot their Korean. Hyung Goo's father was a graduate student, and spoke good English; his mother worked a variety of jobs outside the home, and acquired English that was at least serviceable. Later in life, however, she spent less time in English-speaking environments and more time with Korean-speaking relatives. Over the course of our marriage, her English deteriorated to the point that I could scarcely carry on a conversation with her, and even Hyung Goo had difficulty sometimes in understanding her. Toward the end of Hyung Goo's life, she wrote him several letters in Korean, which we could not read and had to have translated.

Hyung Goo thus ended his life with, quite literally, no mother tongue. He had forgotten his first language, and spoke his second with something other than native fluency.

This sense of having no real home characterized Hyung Goo's entire experience of life. He asked me once, early in our relationship, "Do you think the world is a friendly place?" I was flummoxed by his question. I had never thought about it. But he had, and the answer was a definite no. He had been a child of three when his father traveled to America on a student visa, leaving Hyung Goo, his two brothers, and his mother on their own in Seoul. His mother worked long hours in an effort to support the family. Sometimes a relative supervised the children in her absence; sometimes no one did. They lived first in a two-room house with an outhouse in the front yard, and later in a single room behind a fish market. The room had no door, and in winter they hung a blanket in the opening to cut down the draft. Occasionally Hyung Goo's mother would tell the children that they had to skip a meal in order to take some medicine. Later he realized that these were occasions when she had no food to feed them.

The Immigration Act of 1964 eased restrictions to immigration that had been in place since the 1920s. In December of 1964, Hyung Goo and his brothers, now ages 5, 7, and 9, along with their mother, joined their father in Boston. Hyung Goo's father was surprised when the sons he had not seen in four years failed to show him the complete and unquestioning obedience that he remembered according his own father. His sons, who had been essentially raising themselves, were surprised that anyone, least of all this complete stranger, should expect to tell them what to do. The family settled in Waltham, a western suburb of Boston and the home of Brandeis University, where Hyung Goo's father was working on a Ph.D. They lived in a public housing project that was safe and full of children. Hyung Goo and his brothers attended public schools. A few years later, their sister, Grace, was born, an event that "changed all our lives for the better," Hyung Goo said later.

Hyung Goo loved school. He was interested in every subject, and did well in all of them. By the end of second grade, he had caught up with his peers in his command of the English language. By the fourth grade, he had decided he wanted to go to Harvard. He was recognized by his teachers as one of the brightest students they had ever encountered. In subject after subject, he was offered opportunities for individual instruction. In a connection we discovered years later, his ninth-grade ancient history teacher had herself been taught by my grandfather at Boston University. She wrote in his yearbook that he had been her most rewarding student to teach in many years. He excelled in nonacademic areas as well. He was an athlete. He played the violin. He was involved in student government.

And he was quietly, desperately unhappy. Although he never lacked for friends, he felt socially awkward and insecure. In the seventh grade, he began to suffer from insomnia. Beginning a habit that would continue for years, he would get up in the middle of the night, climb down from the porch roof outside his bedroom window, and wander around for hours, alone in the night, until he was exhausted. Halfway through high school he dropped his involvement in sports, and received his coaches' expressions of disappointment as indications that he was not a trustworthy or dependable person. His schoolwork began to suffer. He had trouble writing. He scraped by in his classes, earning A's out of native intelligence rather than real work.

Despite his academic problems, he entered Harvard in the fall of 1976 thinking of himself as a hotshot. After all, he reasoned, his college board scores were significantly higher than the average at Harvard. Later he realized he would have done better to attend a school where he might have received some of the support he needed. At Harvard, the rule was sink or swim, and Hyung Goo sank. His study habits were not equal to the demands of the physics major he had declared. He fell hopelessly behind in his classes. He was desperately lonely, and terrified of rejection. He became sexually involved with other men, seeing these anonymous encounters as the only available means of satisfying his sexual urges. He participated in the college-age group at Park Street Church, and the disconnect between his Christian confession and his promiscuous behavior weighed on him.

After nearly flunking out each of his first three semesters, Hyung Goo left school to regroup. He consulted a psychiatrist, who diagnosed major depression and prescribed medication and psychotherapy. Two years later, he reenrolled, only to drop out late in the semester. The next time he sought readmission, he was required to undergo a battery of psychological tests. This time the diagnosis was mild bipolar disorder. This certainly squared with his behavior in the intervening years, which had included manic episodes of madly chasing after women, interspersed with depressive episodes of anonymous sex with men. He finally returned to Harvard in the fall of 1984, and graduated in November of 1986 with a major in biochemistry. In the meantime, he had tested positive for HIV. He had hoped

25

to go on to medical school. His positive HIV status made that dream seem impractical at best, and he took a research job at Massachusetts General Hospital. Work became his main reason for living, and he spent long hours at the lab. He was still working in this lab when we started dating, three years later.

In 1937, the sociologist Everett Stonequist coined the term "marginal man." The marginal man, said Stonequist, is "one who is poised in psychological uncertainty between two or more social worlds, reflecting in his soul the discords and harmonies, repulsions and attractions of these worlds." Stonequist was talking about the experience of racial minorities in white-majority America, and in this sense Hyung Goo, as a Korean immigrant, certainly fit his definition. But Hyung Goo was a marginal man in more dimensions than this. He dwelt in a liminal region between homosexuality and heterosexuality, between psychopathology and psychological health, between Christian faith and a rejection of that faith; and, after his HIV diagnosis, between the land of the dead and the land of the living. Perhaps most fundamentally of all, he lived at the edge of despair and longed for joy.

"Do you think the world is a friendly place?" It was a long time before I began to understand the profound sadness and longing that underlay this question. In retrospect, I realize that I shared both his sadness and his longing. I had suffered from them much less dramatically than he had, and I was then much less aware of these poles of my experience than he was. But I was drawn to Hyung Goo as strongly and as quickly as I was at least in part because, in a way I could not then begin to articulate, I sensed that with him I could be at home as I had never been at home before.

The wonder of our marriage was that together we came home. Because of the specter of Hyung Goo's illness, which hung over us all the days of our marriage, we were never able to imagine that this home was anything other than the home a pilgrim has, a shelter on the journey. And yet it was a shelter for the two of us together. Together we found ourselves as man and woman, husband and wife, companions in everything life

26

had to offer, recipients together of more joy than either of us had imagined possible.

Home turned out to be a place where a lot of Korean food was served. The first time Hyung Goo's mother set a plate of Korean food before me, I thought, "Hmm." As a wedding gift, she gave me a rice cooker that seemed enormous and unnecessary. Hadn't I been cooking rice perfectly successfully in a saucepan for years? It wasn't long before I was using that rice cooker nearly every day, and would no more have thought of cooking rice in a saucepan than of doing laundry in the bathtub. Our pantry was stocked with twenty-pound bags of rice, packages of buckwheat noodles, hot bean paste, dried shrimp, black beans. There were rice noodles in the freezer, and jars of kimchee in the fridge. I never did come to like kimchee myself, and I required Hyung Goo to keep the jars swathed in multiple layers of plastic, in a never entirely successful attempt to keep everything else in the refrigerator from becoming kimchee-flavored.

I spent the Christmas after Hyung Goo's death with his relatives in Boston. At dinner I helped myself from the usual holiday assortment of dishes, cleaned my plate, and went back for more. "Hey," I thought. "This is really good."

A couple of months later I was in New York, where Hyung Goo and I had a favorite Korean restaurant. I had dinner there, taking along two of my brothers and my sister-in-law. They had never had Korean food, so I ordered for us, explaining the menu and demonstrating how to use the tabletop barbecue grill and how to assemble and eat the various dishes. "Hey," they said. "This is really good."

Those two meals form a sort of parable of Hyung Goo's gift to me. All during our marriage, I had thought I was learning to like Korean food for his sake. Only after his death did I realize that it hadn't just been for him, or even for us. It had been for me, for my relationships with his relatives, with my relatives, with our friends in New York, in Boston, in Durham, across the country and around the world.

I married Hyung Goo feeling that here at last was the companion I had longed for all my life. I spent our entire marriage mourning the fact that when he died, I would be alone again. But when he died, I was not alone again. I was a widow, to be sure, and I grieved for him and for our lost life with an intensity that startled even me. But I found myself in the midst of a vast web of connections that in some mysterious way had been woven from the very liminality of Hyung Goo's existence. As a man living on the margins, who felt himself always on the outside looking in, he reached out for deep and intimate connection with me, and in so doing transformed me and my fractured experience of the world.

# MARCH 17, 1990:
# STARTING AZT

The first drug that was developed specifically to treat HIV infection was called Azidothymidine, or AZT for short. Previously, some of the symptoms of AIDS had been treatable, but the underlying cause had not been. Now, there was a drug that acted to suppress HIV itself. AZT and AIDS quickly became nearly synonymous with one another, as clinicians and patients attempted to establish appropriate dosages and to understand the possibilities and limitations of treatment with AZT. Should AZT be prescribed as soon as a person was known to be HIV-positive? Should treatment (with its high cost and attendant side effects) be delayed until symptoms of disease had appeared? A typical compromise was to prescribe AZT when an HIV-infected person was still apparently healthy, but the level of a certain kind of white blood cell, the T4 or CD4 lymphocyte, indicated that the immune system had begun to be damaged.

This happened for Hyung Goo in March of 1990, five years after he had first tested positive for HIV. We had been dating only a few months, and I was trying to imagine whether I could marry someone who one day would be ill with AIDS. Now, with Hyung Goo's CD4 count below 500, and a bottle of AZT in his possession, it seemed to me that, for all practical purposes, he had AIDS already. Each blue-banded capsule was a reminder, renewed five times a day, of impending doom: "You're not sick yet, but you will be one day." Hyung Goo did not see it this way.

29

For him, as for so many others with AIDS or HIV, AZT was an icon, not of doom, but of hope. "I look at it as something that may keep me from getting sick at all," he said.

In fact, AZT did not keep Hyung Goo from getting sick. That day in March of 1990 proved to be the beginning of a long journey through the thicket of AIDS medications. It seemed that Hyung Goo must have taken every single one of them at one time or another: drugs to treat HIV infection itself, drugs to treat opportunistic infections, drugs as prophylaxis against other opportunistic infections, drugs for fever, drugs for pain, drugs to combat the side effects of other medications. Hyung Goo spent hours talking with his physicians as they tried together to make sense of his symptoms and his medications and their side effects and interactions.

The crescendo of medication grew only slowly at first. For a year and a half, AZT was Hyung Goo's only AIDS-related medication. We married in the spring of 1991 and he joined me in Durham, where he became a patient at the Duke Infectious Diseases Clinic. His physician there started him on aerosolized Pentamidine as prophylaxis against PCP, an AIDS-related pneumonia. Once a month, Hyung Goo would go to the treatment room at the clinic and breathe in a fine mist of medication through a special apparatus, in the hope that this would fend off the advent of PCP.

In the spring of 1992, Hyung Goo's CD4 count fell below 200, which indicated that his immune system was now seriously damaged. By this time new antiretroviral drugs—that is, drugs that, like AZT, aimed at suppressing HIV itself—were becoming available. Hyung Goo's doctor started him on one of these, Didanosine, or ddI. DdI was a lot of trouble to take. It came as tablets that had to be crushed to powder with a mortar and pestle, and then mixed with water and drunk on an empty stomach twice a day. DdI turned out to be correlated with depression, and for Hyung Goo, who hovered on the border of depression even under the best of circumstances, this was not good. Eventually he stopped taking ddI, concluding that it wasn't worth the trouble or the side effects.

That fall, Hyung Goo was diagnosed with Kaposi's sarcoma, a kind of tumor of the capillaries. Initially, a few of the KS lesions were treated with topical injections of the drug Vincristine. This damaged so much of the surrounding healthy tissue that Hyung Goo decided he would rather just leave the lesions alone. A year later the KS had progressed to the point that treatment with intravenous Vincristine was recommended. Hyung Goo had his first dose of this as an outpatient just before Thanksgiving of 1993, and felt thoroughly miserable for several weeks afterward. It turned out that his sensitivity to the drug was so great that he could not tolerate a conventional dose of it. Treatment was postponed, and later resumed at a greatly decreased dosage.

Sometime around the time of Hyung Goo's initial KS diagnosis, in the fall of 1992, another of his blood counts fell to a dangerous level. This time it was his neutrophils, a kind of white cell involved in fighting bacterial infections. In an effort to raise that count, he began taking a growth factor called Neupogen, or GCSF (Granulocyte Colony Stimulating Factor). Hyung Goo gave himself injections of Neupogen twice a week. He would sit at the dining-room table after dinner, with his syringes and various other bits of equipment spread out before him and his pants around his ankles, and inject the drug into his belly or thigh. As anemia became a problem, he began to receive transfusions of packed red blood cells at the clinic every few weeks. Eventually he added another growth factor, one called Epogen (Erythropoietin, or Epo for short). This, too, was administered by subcutaneous injection, also at the dinner table.

The drug regimen took a dramatic turn for the more complex in January of 1994, when Hyung Goo was diagnosed with CMV (Cytomegalovirus), an infection of the eye which, untreated, leads to blindness. Treatment required the daily administration of Ganciclovir, a drug that could be taken only intravenously. A temporary IV line was put in Hyung Goo's hand the day he was diagnosed with CMV; a few days later he had a permanent IV catheter implanted in his chest. Hyung Goo took Ganciclovir once or twice a day for the rest of his life, with the exception of

31

two weeks during which his physicians tried switching him to another medication, Foscarnet, which he proved spectacularly unable to tolerate.

Not too long after his initial diagnosis with CMV, Hyung Goo began to run fevers. These turned out to be symptomatic of PCP, the AIDS-related pneumonia as prophylaxis against which he had been taking aerosolized Pentamidine for years. The treatment of choice for PCP was Bactrim, a sulfa drug, but Hyung Goo was allergic to sulfa. Another possibility was intravenous Pentamidine, but this was associated with various unattractive side effects, like loss of appetite and nausea. Hyung Goo and his doctor decided to try a newer drug, Mepron, and see how it worked. Mepron was a bright yellow, opaque liquid, like yellow paint, that was taken by mouth. It turned out not to be a great drug for PCP. Hyung Goo did get better, but when he discontinued treatment, the PCP would return, and need to be beaten back again. After months of this, he ended up on IV Pentamidine, with all its nasty side effects. Even this turned out not to be sufficient to keep PCP at bay forever.

In the summer of 1994 we spent a number of weeks in Boston, at which time we consulted with several physicians, including a team at Beth Israel Hospital who specialized in the treatment of Kaposi's sarcoma. We came away from a four-and-a-half hour conversation with the doctors and nurses there with our heads spinning. Should Hyung Goo's KS be treated as it had been at Duke? They didn't think so, mainly because Hyung Goo was so sensitive to the drugs used that he could tolerate them only in very small doses. Perhaps it could be treated with Velban and Bleomycin, or, assuming they could find a clinical trial for which he was eligible, with one of the new, experimental, liposomal products (I never did find out what these were). What about the nausea associated with the KS treatment? There were half a dozen options for how to treat that; they settled on 30 mg of time-release Compazine twice a day, supplemented by regular Compazine as needed.

Then there was the painkiller question. They thought Hyung Goo was taking too much Tylenol for his liver to handle, and should go on a morphine derivative instead. Much conversation ensued about how much to take, and when, and what to do about the other purposes that Tylenol served, like fever reduction. Then there were his blood counts, which kept dropping, but why? Was it a result of HIV infection itself? Was it all the chemotherapy drugs he was taking? Or was it another opportunistic infection, like MAI (*Mycobacterium avium*)? They didn't know. They took blood to culture for MAI, and planned to continue transfusions as needed for the four to six weeks it would take to get results from the culture. And what about Hyung Goo's PCP? It kept coming back because he was taking Mepron for it instead of Bactrim, to which he was allergic; but perhaps he could try a desensitization treatment that was sometimes used for sulfa allergies, starting with a minuscule dose and moving up over three weeks' time to a full dose.

And so the conversation went, on and on and on. That evening I wrote to my therapist, "What do people do who haven't got the kind of mental equipment we do for dealing with all this information? I suppose one answer is that their doctors don't tell them as much. Maybe another answer is that they die sooner because they can't participate in their own care. But all I can say is, I am trying to understand and remember more than I am equipped to understand and remember, and it is crushing me."

The following October, we spent a long weekend in Iowa visiting friends and relatives. While we were there, Hyung Goo noticed large numbers of floaters in his right eye. Fearing a retinal detachment, we ended up at University Hospitals in Iowa City on a Sunday, where he was examined by an ophthalmologist. Before doing the examination, the ophthalmologist took a history, which included questions about what medications Hyung Goo was currently taking. We hardly knew where to begin. From then on, I kept a list in my wallet, written on the back of a checking account deposit slip, of all Hyung Goo's current medications and dosages. If we found ourselves in an emergency room or talking to a new doctor, we could just take out the list and read it off, instead of scrambling to remember everything that was on it. That list, with its scribbled updates, became so accustomed a part of the contents of my wallet that it was months after Hyung Goo's death before I could bring myself to take it out.

In the summer of 1995, expanded clinical trials were announced for a promising new class of antiretroviral drugs, protease inhibitors. Lotteries were held to select participants in the clinical trials, and Hyung Goo was selected to participate in the trial of the Merck drug, Crixivan. "Wouldn't it be wonderful if it actually worked?" he said to me. Yes, it would be wonderful. I could feel myself hoping with him, knowing full well his prognosis, and yet hoping for longer, healthier life, daring to imagine that it might be possible. Perhaps we could travel at Christmastime; perhaps Hyung Goo would feel better; perhaps we would have more time together; perhaps, perhaps, perhaps.

I remembered Hyung Goo's comment, more than five years earlier: "I look at AZT as something that may keep me from getting sick at all." At the time, this had seemed to me utterly unrealistic. Indeed, one of our pastors had interpreted Hyung Goo's comment as denial: Hyung Goo didn't think he was going to die of AIDS, but we all knew better. I was angry with the conclusion this pastor drew—that this was yet another reason I should not marry Hyung Goo—but I more than half agreed with him that Hyung Goo was "in denial." Isn't any kind of hope for health and long life in a person who has a terminal illness "denial"? Shouldn't such a person be encouraged to take a thoroughly bleak view of his future, as bleak a view as his friends and associates may be inclined to take?

I realized now how different things look when you are the one whose health and life are threatened, and something appears on the horizon that seems to suggest that perhaps you, too, can have a future that includes good things. All our married life, I had been the one who thought that if Hyung Goo wasn't dying today, he probably would be tomorrow; while Hyung Goo, all the time dealing with the ever-increasing medical routine, had clung doggedly to the belief that if he was okay today, he could be okay tomorrow. But now, if ever so briefly, my heart had lifted with his at the idea that maybe this new medication would actually do some good, and we would have more time. This was not denial; it was hope: engagement with reality as it was and as it might be.

Protease inhibitors turned out to effect dramatic improvements in the health of at least some of the patients who were able both to afford them and to tolerate them, but they came a little too late for Hyung Goo. If he had qualified for the Crixivan trial, which depended on his having a platelet count above a certain level, he might have begun participation by the end of that year. But he died in September, before the trial began, and perhaps it was just as well. Protease inhibitors are complex drugs to take and tolerate, and Hyung Goo was so sick by that time that it might just have been too much to attempt.

The day after Hyung Goo died, the telephone rang with an inquiry from the home-health company that had been providing the intravenous drug used to treat Hyung Goo's eye condition. What supplies did we need? I told them we didn't need any, and why. They sent the delivery person over to pick up all the Ganciclovir and IV supplies that Hyung Goo already had. Hyung Goo's social worker offered to come by and take away the rest of the leftover medication. A week or two later I sat down to go through it all before she came for it.

There was a lot of it. I calculated about 12,000 capsules or tablets of prescription medication—some of it current, some of it not—plus several thousand more of various over-the-counter drugs. Drugs for PCP, HIV, MAC, thrush, nausea, ulcers, sleep, fever, pain. Mepron, Bactrim, Biaxin, Mycelex, Compazine, Diflucan, Cipro, Dilaudid, Reglan, MSContin, Rifabutin, 3TC, Valium, Zofran, Ceftin, Zantac, Prilosec, Ethambutol, Lamprene, Amitryptylene, Tylox, Ibuprofen, five or six different kinds of Tylenol, not to mention sixty-two vials each of Neupogen and Epogen in the refrigerator. And, of course, AZT. I sorted through all of it; I counted out the pills; I made lists of them and gathered all the bottles together on the dining-room table and took a picture of them.

Even as I was doing this, it seemed obsessive. Later that evening, it dawned on me: this was what Hyung Goo would have done. He would never have handed over his medication before going through all of it and making sure he knew what

35

was there. If he had been there to do it himself, I would have thought it a waste of time and energy—we were giving the medicine away because we didn't need it, so who cared how much of it there was? But in his absence, my instinctive and completely unreflective, unconscious impulse was to do what he would have done.

It took longer to realize that sorting through the medicine was a symbolic beginning to the long process of trying to make sense of the life that Hyung Goo and I had had together. I went through the physical remains of that life, precisely because it was over. I needed to know what it had been before I could think about anything else. I went through the Christmas card list, categorizing everyone on it according to how he or she had come to be part of my life, trying to bring everyone into view before I started trying to figure out which relationships to move forward with, and which ones to lay to rest. I pulled all the clothes out of the closet, discarding some of my own and keeping a few of his, even as I gave away great armloads of Hyung Goo's clothes to friends whom I hoped they would fit. I sorted through masses and masses of insurance paperwork, all meticulously recorded and annotated by Hyung Goo, who had kept track of it all.

And I told and retold the stories of Hyung Goo's and my marriage, and of his illness and death, to anyone and everyone who would listen, over and over and over again, trying somehow to figure out what, after all, the story was, and what it all meant. How, from such small beginnings, had we grown into such fullness? How could such fullness have been so heartbreaking? Compared with these questions, the multiplication of that first bottle of AZT into the profusion of leftover medicine seemed simple indeed. But if the medicine could be corralled, maybe the rest of the story could be figured out, too. Perhaps this is why I still find it faintly reassuring to have that photograph of all the medicine, 119 bottles of it, neatly lined up on the blue-and-white-checked dining-room tablecloth. That, at least, is nicely organized.

# SCHOOL DAZE

I was in graduate school at Duke during the whole of Hyung Goo's and my marriage. Under different circumstances, school might have been the primary focus of my attention in those years. As it was, I was completely wrapped up in Hyung Goo and our life together, and graduate study came in a distant second. It wouldn't be quite accurate to say that I got a Ph.D. in my spare time, but it wouldn't be too far off the mark, either. It is certainly true that my formation as a theologian, a scholar, and a teacher was deeply affected by my concurrent experiences of marriage and of grief.

I had imagined that the beginning of my doctoral program would mark the end of my relationship with Hyung Goo. I had told him I couldn't marry him, and I saw the move to North Carolina as an opportunity to make a clean break and start over. But Hyung Goo, not content just to wave goodbye, insisted on driving my rental moving van to Durham for me. Since I had little confidence in my ability to drive a fifteen-foot truck with my car on a tow dolly behind it, I didn't feel I was in a very good position to refuse his help.

The day we arrived in Durham, Hyung Goo developed a stomachache. A few days later he flew home, taking with him a bottle of antacid that, fortunately, he never used. The next day I got a call from his father. While on the plane, Hyung Goo had realized that his stomachache was not indigestion; it was appendicitis. When he arrived in Boston, he retrieved his car, drove to the hospital, and had an emergency appendectomy. I was horrified, and was immediately on the phone with him in his hospital room. So much for my determination just to forget about Hyung Goo.

Even apart from the appendix episode, I doubt very much that I would have been able to follow through on my resolve just to get on with my life. As it was, I was immediately as preoccupied with Hyung Goo as I had ever been. Midway through my first semester at Duke I realized that maybe I did want to marry Hyung Goo after all. The remainder of the school year was taken up with deciding to get married and planning the wedding. I kept a bridal magazine in my briefcase, and took it out and studied it during class breaks. When the break was over, I put it away and busied myself with drawing little pictures in the margins of my notes of where members of the bridal party were to stand in the church during the ceremony. The following school year we were newlyweds, and the several school years after that were taken up with trying to live as fully as we could, as fast as we could, in the little time we had.

As a result of all this preoccupation, I never really engaged with my doctoral program as I might have done, and as it seemed most of my fellow students did. Part of graduate school is being socialized into the life of the academy: getting to know who the major players are, figuring out where the lines of loyalty are drawn, and deciding where you want to stand. But I didn't want to stand anywhere. I was very ambivalent about being in graduate school at all. I genuinely wanted a Ph.D., because I wanted to teach, and a Ph.D. is a required credential for a teaching career. And I wanted to study theology, because theology is about everything, and I liked thinking about everything. But I was also very angry that my world was not as I wished it to be, and I was full of existential anxiety about life and death and Hyung Goo and me and what might happen and whether we would be up for it.

I tried to lessen the anxiety by adopting an aloof and dismissive attitude in my classes. In the advanced theology seminar, faculty and students engaged in spirited and seemingly endless conversations about Derrida, Foucault, Milbank, Deleuze, Polanyi, structuralism, foundationalism, deconstructionism, postmodernism, and several other isms, while I sat looking bored and irritated. "When your husband is dying of AIDS," I thought crossly to myself, "who cares about any of this?" But no one knew Hyung Goo had AIDS until a couple of years later, by which time I was finished with my coursework and well into writing my dissertation. All anyone knew was what they could see: that I seemed to have little but contempt for my studies. I doubt that this won me any friends; and in the end, it did nothing to reduce my anxiety either. The primary result was that I didn't learn nearly as much theology as I might have.

The anger I took out on Stanley Hauerwas. Stanley, one of the theologians on the Duke faculty, was a person of strong convictions and equally strong personality. He was a pacifist who was profoundly critical of the unthinking equation, made by many, between being an American and being a Christian. He also swore like a sailor, and tended to voice all his opinions at the top of his lungs. On warm and otherwise quiet evenings, when the windows of the divinity school were open, you could hear Stanley yelling at his classes from across the quad. Faculty and students alike tended to love Stanley or to hate him. I despised him. At the time, I thought I had principled reasons for doing so. In fact, my dislike of him had very little to do with principle, and everything to do with me. I had one class with Stanley, an ethics class that included fifty or sixty master's-level divinity students, and a handful of doctoral students. All the doctoral students except me sat together on one side of the room in the front. I sat on the other side of the room in the back, slumped in my seat, with a scowl on my face and cotton in my ears. Public forums were worse. Every time I was at a meeting where Stanley spoke, I had something pointedly critical to say in response.

Stanley, for his part, was mystified. We had never had a conversation, and knew each other only by sight. There was no evident reason for my animus toward him. One day, after another critical public exchange, we encountered one another in the hallway. I glanced at him and walked past. "Why are you always so angry with me?" he demanded. "You could at least say hello." Feeling abashed and provoked in equal measure, I wrote him a letter and offered to talk. He wrote back and agreed to meet. But before we could get together, a mutual friend, foreseeing an explosion that didn't have to happen, went to Stanley and told him about Hyung Goo's illness. Stanley was floored. He had, quite naturally, thought of me as a thoroughly unpleasant and self-centered person. Now I appeared in rather a different light. Our meeting never took place. We had both had the wind taken out of our sails, I by his willingness to talk with me, and he by the discovery that my life was complicated in ways he had not imagined. We tacitly declared a truce; there were no more public confrontations, and no private conversations either. It took me years to realize that, in fact, I liked and respected Stanley and valued the friendship that, as it turned out, he had always been ready to give.

What I lacked in intellectual engagement with my own program the first year I was at Duke, I made up for with my involvement as a tutor in the chemistry department. The reigning myth of organic chemistry is that you have to get an A in it to get into medical school. This creates a steady supply of students eager for tutoring, so when I found I needed income beyond that supplied by my stipend, I became a tutor. The only difficulty was that it had been ten years since my own college class in organic, and I had forgotten it all. I addressed this problem by attending class along with my students every Monday, Wednesday, and Friday morning, and then working all the problems in the book and in the instructor's problem sets before holding any of my tutorial sessions.

That organic chemistry class proved less marginal to my graduate program than one might have expected. In the short run, it allowed me to spend a lot of time working chemistry problems, which were concrete, mathematical, spatial, and utterly different from theology, with its endless reflection on the meaning of life. I was in a graduate program in theology because I wanted to think about the meaning of life, but just then my own life was presenting me with more than enough opportunities to do so. Chemistry served as a safety valve, something I could exercise my mind on and be conveyed far, far away from preoccupations with Hyung Goo and HIV and the consummate unfairness of it all.

In the long run, the class served as a seminar in pedagogy. It was taught by a professor emeritus who, it turned out, was teaching the year-long organic chemistry sequence for the last time. Pelham Wilder had been at Duke for nearly forty years, and he had refined his lectures and problem sets until each was a work of art, illustrating each point he wished to make with precision and elegance. Because I had studied the subject previously and was attending class for review, I was in a position to pay attention not only to what he was saying, but also to how he was saying it, and to recognize the choices he was making as he ordered and selected his material. Each class was the performance of a master, and gave me an example to aspire to as I contemplated my own future as a teacher.

Eventually I did start paying attention to my own graduate program. I learned a great deal from the historians David Steinmetz and Grant Wacker, and the theologian Geoffrey Wainwright, as I participated in their graduate seminars and served as a teaching assistant in their divinity school classes. Geoffrey Wainwright was my advisor. His accomplishments as a theologian were enhanced by his rhetorical gifts, as I learned at one of the first social events I attended at Duke, the annual beginning-of-the-year reception for faculty and students in the graduate program in religion. During a pause in the conversation, faculty members were invited to introduce themselves. The first person to speak was a scholar of Akkadian. "I'm so-and-so, and I teach dead languages," he said, to general laughter.

Next was an archaeologist. "I'm so-and-so, and I teach dead civilizations." More laughter.

Then it was Wainwright's turn. "I'm Geoffrey Wainwright, and I teach the living tradition."

In addition to these several friends on the faculty, I made a few good friends among my fellow students, and had a nodding acquaintance with various other students and faculty members. But there were many people whom I never got to know, and as Hyung Goo got sicker, I withdrew further and further from any visible involvement at school. Hyung Goo died at the beginning of my sixth year at Duke. The following spring, there was a reception for prospective students in the graduate program in religion. Faculty and current students were invited to come and meet people who had been accepted to the program for the following year. When I arrived at the reception, I was startled to find that I recognized practically no one, having no idea who were the current students (or even faculty) and who were the prospective ones. Even I hadn't realized until then just how out of circulation I had been, and for how long.

My disengagement with my academic work, and my excruciatingly slow progress on my dissertation, had in fact been a major source of conflict between Hyung Goo and me. Hyung Goo wanted more than anything else to know that I would be okay after he was gone, and having a Ph.D. and being able to support myself in an academic career was a big part of being okay. We had also moved to Durham, far from family and friends in Boston, specifically so that I could be in graduate school at Duke, and we both needed to believe that it was my dissertation, rather than Hyung Goo's medical needs alone, that kept us there. On the other hand, while I was happy enough to maintain continuing status in my program, and to do a little bit of work here and there, I thought the dissertation would keep, whereas Hyung Goo wouldn't. I preferred to give my attention to him, and to worry about finishing the Ph.D. later. In the last year or so of our marriage, especially, I felt increasingly caught between what I could do and what Hyung Goo wanted me to do. Hyung Goo sensed the tide ebbing out, and wanted me to work hard and fast on the dissertation, so that he could see me finish before he died. I could sense the tide ebbing out, too, and was so anxious I could barely think. I felt utterly defeated by the dissertation, and simultaneously that I was failing Hyung Goo every day that I didn't accomplish something on it.

During that last year of Hyung Goo's life, I applied for several academic positions. I had no business doing so, as I was only in the beginning stages of my dissertation. But every graduate student imagines he or she will be finished long before finishing is a realistic possibility, and Hyung Goo wanted very much for me to have a job as soon as possible. To our surprise, I was offered an interview at one of the schools to which I had applied. I traveled to the interview in March of 1995. From one perspective it was a complete fiasco. Not only did I not get the job, I landed in the middle of a power struggle that had nothing to do with me, and by the time the dust had settled, several months later, there had been angry meetings and resignations and articles in the newspaper.

From another perspective, it was the best thing that could have happened. I made several lasting friendships with members of the search committee, I learned a lot about academic politics, and Hyung Goo realized that I would be just fine. As his social worker said to me later, he hadn't just wanted to know where I would get a job; he wanted to read my contract and meet my boss and inspect my office and generally chaperone me into whatever my position was. The interview experience let him relax his grip on all that, as he saw me learn to hold my own in the midst of academia at its most tumultuous. Hyung Goo died that fall. He would have loved to have seen me finish; he would have loved to have known where I would end up; but he wasn't worried any more. He knew I would be okay.

I resumed work on the dissertation after the new year. I had realized within weeks of Hyung Goo's death that I would know when it was time to start writing again, and that when the time came, I would do it and it would get done. I wasn't accomplishing any more on the dissertation than I had been before, but I didn't feel demoralized by it any longer. I made arrangements not to serve as a teaching assistant in the spring, in order to have more time to devote to my own work. I reported my plans to Hyung Goo's social worker, who was delighted with my new sense of purpose. "Hyung Goo knew this. He knew it," she said, and paused. "Most of him did." And we both laughed almost until we cried. She was right. Hyung Goo had boundless confidence in me, but he had a few little worries around the edges, too, which formed part of his solicitude for me—so sweet, and so touching.

It took me another couple of years to finish. I took a job as a college professor, and began teaching the church history I had learned from David Steinmetz, and the theology I had learned from Geoffrey Wainwright. And I have continued to hold my academic career at arm's length, much as I did my graduate studies for so many years at Duke. Then I did so partly out of anxious exhaustion, and partly in the conviction that what I was doing at home was at least as important as anything I might do at school. Now that the exhaustion of grief, and the subsequent exhaustion of beginning a teaching career, have mostly subsided, I have more energy for teaching and reading and writing than I ever had before. But I still find that my primary allegiance is to home. I have a different family now, but we need dinner on the table in the evening just as much as Hyung Goo and I did. God is in the details, said T. S. Eliot. Is it possible to be a theologian while giving most of one's attention to the details of housekeeping? I hope so.

# LEARNING TO DANCE

Hyung Goo and I were married on a beautifully sunny Saturday in June of 1991. I wore my great-grandmother's wedding dress of tissue-thin Paris muslin and inset lace over layers of crinoline petticoats. The bridesmaids' dresses were pink flowered cotton, and had been made by various relatives in an effort at economy. Fortunately, only two of the six got made with the pattern upside down. Even more fortunately, the pattern was small enough that it didn't really matter. We had asked for flowers that were local and in season, and the florist responded with arrangements overflowing with peonies and roses and delphiniums. "I feel like I'm hiding behind a bush," my matron of honor said as she held up her bouquet. Hyung Goo and his groomsmen wore cutaway coats and striped trousers. Friends from the chorus sang Purcell, Mozart, and Brahms; the organist played Bach and Vaughan Williams. Hundreds of friends and relatives filled the pews.

That wedding felt like such a triumph. We felt like we had already been through the wars together, and getting married was the culmination, the high point, and in a sense the end. Later it seemed that our life together began the day we got married, and that everything leading up to that day was only a prelude to the real thing.

We had, of course, no idea what we were getting into. We thought we did, in that we had recited our wedding vows—"in sickness and in health, until death do us part"—in the knowledge that that was exactly what we were promising. But those words describe only external circumstances, and no marriage is equivalent to its external circumstances. Being married is like dancing, and the size and shape of the room don't tell you much about the dance itself. At our wedding, we announced our choice of partner. It remained to discover what the steps to the dance were, to trip all over one another's feet in the process of learning to do them, and then finally to have practiced enough that we no longer needed to concentrate on the mechanics and could relax and let the dance unfold, carrying us with it through arabesques that now embodied our life together as husband and wife.

We had all the same steps to learn that any couple does. One of the first things that dawned on us was that we had married each other, in all our particularity, rather than some ideal or generic version of a husband or a wife. In some respects this was obvious. We learned quickly that when we wrote our names together, it was important that my name come first: "Margaret and Hyung Goo Kim." If we wrote "Hyung Goo and Margaret Kim," we got back mail addressed, "Dear Mr. Goo and Ms. Kim."

Other things took longer to figure out. I had a happily married friend who had always made a point of ironing her husband's shirts. Almost intentionally, I took her as a model. She was a good wife and she ironed her husband's shirts; I would be a good wife and iron my husband's shirts, too. But Hyung Goo didn't want his shirts ironed. He had always just hung them up after taking them out of the dryer, and he thought it was a waste of time for anyone to iron them. He didn't really care whether I ironed my own shirts, but he was genuinely irritated when he found me ironing his. It actually took me quite a while to relinquish my fantasy ideal of the good wife as one who irons her husband's shirts, in favor of a recognition that the person I was actually married to preferred his shirts wrinkled.

The most regular routines of our life revolved around food. I wanted us to sit down to dinner together every evening, and conflated this desire with the idea that dinner should always be at the same time: 6:00, say. But Hyung Goo was a scientist, and his experiments didn't always end tidily at 5:30. He was used to staying at the lab until all hours, and stopping for Chinese food on the way home. We both compromised. He agreed to come home for dinner, and I agreed that dinner would be when he came home. Hyung Goo would call to let me know when to expect him, and I would have dinner on the table when he arrived.

At first, we ate off old mismatched china plates covered with pink peacocks, with old silverplate flatware that had worn through to the base metal underneath. Both plates and flatware had belonged to my grandparents, and while they were a homely lot, to me they felt comfortably familiar. Hyung Goo loathed the pink peacocks, and he was sure we were going to be poisoned by the base metal of the flatware. We were on the point of purchasing new dishes and flatware when I remembered our wedding china and silver. It was all just sitting in a cupboard. Why not use it? I packed away the pink peacocks, and got out the bone china and sterling. We ate off our wedding china every day for the rest of our marriage, although we did eventually retire the sterling silver in favor of a set of stainless flatware that our credit-card company gave us after we had charged tens of thousands of dollars worth of medication during one of their promotional periods.

Food itself became a source of conflict as Hyung Goo got sicker. He began coming home from work too tired to eat. He lost weight. His medications nauseated him. Everything tasted like cardboard. I decided that it would be a good idea for me to be in charge of what he ate. If he would just eat what I thought he should eat, when I thought he should eat it, then he would be okay. Hyung Goo's opinion was that he wasn't nearly as sick as I thought he was. He had the situation under control, he would eat what and when he wanted to, and if not eating was what it took to make his point, then he wouldn't eat. On at least a couple of occasions, I ended up on the phone with his social worker, frantic because Hyung Goo wouldn't eat when or what I thought he should. Her response: "He's a big boy. Leave him alone."

Slowly, I began to learn that it was my job to set the food before him, and his job to decide whether or not to eat it. As I stopped trying to control what he ate, he stopped trying to assert control by not eating. Eventually we got to the point that I could try to coax him to eat while recognizing that it was still his decision, and he could allow himself to be coaxed without feeling dominated or infantilized. Intimacy, it turns out, has a great deal to do with recognizing boundaries and respecting them. When you know your spouse is not going to try to barge in on your private space, you are much more likely to let him or her in of your own accord.

I was genuinely surprised to discover that when I was angry with Hyung Goo, he was usually angry with me, too, and usually not without reason. About three years into our marriage, we had a dramatically explosive argument over whether to get a pager. Hyung Goo had been ill with pneumonia a few months earlier, and a physician friend had lent us his pager. The pager made it possible for me to go in to school and yet know that Hyung Goo could reach me at any time. We used it a good deal. When our friend returned from vacation and reclaimed his pager, I wanted to get one of our own. But Hyung Goo didn't want a pager. His pneumonia was in abeyance, he felt fine, and he didn't think it was necessary. I wanted one anyway. I thought it would make me feel calmer, and I didn't care whether Hyung Goo thought it was necessary. The more I pressed to get one, the more adamantly he refused. We went round and round, with me getting madder and madder, until I was so angry I could hardly see straight. We ended up in his social worker's office with me yelling at Hyung Goo while he and the social worker looked at each other, mouthing, "I've never seen her this mad in my life."

Hyung Goo was rather shaken by this whole episode. He gave in, and we got the pager. But as the scene in the social worker's office unfolded, it became apparent that I wasn't only, or even primarily, angry with him because he didn't want a pager. I had been angry my entire life (it turned out) with God, the world, and everyone in it because, it seemed, nobody cared how I felt. I had grown up feeling that no one knew or cared how I felt. God clearly didn't care how I felt, since he was torturing my husband to death while I watched. And when Hyung Goo refused to get a pager on grounds entirely separate from how I felt about it, all that pent-up anger exploded in his direction. All of a sudden it started to become clear why I had been snarling at my therapist every week since I'd started to see him a couple of years previously. It wasn't that he was personally objectionable, but that I was angry. Oh. Hyung Goo was by this time very ready for me to yell at someone besides himself. "Why don't I come with you the next time you see your therapist?" he offered. "I can hold his arms behind his back, and you can punch him in the nose."

It was another year before I began to see Hyung Goo's side of the argument a little more clearly. We were having the stone laid on Hyung Goo's grave, so it would be ready when we needed it, and I had to decide whether I wanted my name on the stone along with his. The alternative was to leave the space for my name blank. I didn't really like to have only his name on the stone, as if he were alone in the world, but I decided to leave mine off. I was only 34, I didn't expect to die anytime soon, and it was just too soon to have my name on a gravestone. Then I remembered why Hyung Goo hadn't wanted a pager. He hadn't wanted one because, to him, a pager meant he was really sick, and he wasn't ready to say that. It was just too soon.

Arguments this tumultuous were few and far between. But nearly every day presented us with one opportunity or another to find ways to live together that were harmonious rather than antagonistic. I liked to make decisions quickly and be done with them; Hyung Goo liked to take his time and keep his options open. I liked to act independently; Hyung Goo liked to be consulted. We both thought it was of the utmost importance to do things "right", and drove each other crazy trying to impose our ideas of rightness on one another. Hyung Goo thought I should downshift at a precise moment while cornering. When I didn't, he would roll his eyes and say, "It's only a transmission." I thought Hyung Goo should wash mushrooms under running water using a brush. When he would dunk them up and down in a basin, I would point at invisible specks of dirt and say, "Look, they're not clean."

Perhaps if we had thought we had more time, we would have dealt with these conflicts as it seemed many of our peers dealt with their marital conflicts: namely, by not dealing with them. Conversations didn't get had, issues didn't get put on the table, resentment simmered unacknowledged, with no opportunity to be aired and resolved. It wasn't that our friends didn't want to get along with one another; it was that they hoped the problems would go away by themselves, just given time. And perhaps they would; but we didn't have time. We couldn't wait until later to be happy together; we had to be happy now, or we'd never be happy. As a result, our sharp edges got smoothed out more quickly than they might have done otherwise. Several years into our marriage, we realized that our marriage had come to seem more like the marriages of our friends who were a generation or two older than ourselves than like the marriages of our peers. We had stopped struggling to make one another into carbon copies of ourselves, and had done so not out of resignation but in acceptance and contentment. Instead of leaning away from one another, each continually tugging at the other and threatening to pull him or her off balance, we began to lean toward each other, supporting rather than destabilizing one another.

A few months before Hyung Goo died we had another argument. I had gone into the study one evening and spent an hour on the phone with a friend. I had thought Hyung Goo was downstairs making the egg drop soup he usually had before bed, and running in his IV medication, which took about an hour. When I came downstairs, I discovered him sitting in front of the television. He hadn't eaten; he hadn't done his medicine. I was thoroughly annoyed. I couldn't even have an hour to myself; I had to be supervising Hyung Goo or nothing would get done. Before I could say anything, he looked at me and said, "Do you want to know why I'm mad at you?"

"Why?" I asked, stifling a scream. He was upset that I had spent an hour on the phone, which seemed to him ridiculously extravagant. I pointed out that this was a friend with whom I seldom got to talk, and left it at that. It was too late, and we were too tired, to talk about it any more. I cooked his soup, he did his medicine, and we went to bed.

The next morning, I was in the kitchen preparing breakfast. Hyung Goo came in and lifted up the teakettle to make sure that I wasn't boiling any more water than necessary for his cup of coffee (inefficiency, you know). "Look, I don't want that to be something else I get yelled at about," I snapped.

Hyung Goo took half a step backwards, cocked his head, paused, and said, "What else do you get yelled at about?"

"Um, well, I guess I'm still upset about that criticism about the phone call last night," I mumbled. "And you hadn't eaten your soup or done your medicine and I was annoyed."

"My poor baby!" he said, holding out his arms. We both started to laugh.

That conversation stands out in my memory as the surest indication we had that we had grown up. Hyung Goo had realized he could deal with my anger, and didn't have to be afraid of it. Instead of bracing himself against it, or hoping that if he ignored it it would go away, he learned to wade right in and engage with it, and with me. And I learned to let him in, to be open even when angry, and not barricade myself behind a snit.

"What else do you get yelled at about?" What I heard was, "I care how you feel; tell me, and I'll make it better." And I did feel better. I felt received, and loved, and cared for. And Hyung Goo, who couldn't begin to fix what we were both really upset about—that he was dying—was not powerless, and he knew it. He knew he could make all the difference in the world to me and to the two of us together. We had learned to be married; we had learned how to dance.

# THE CLINIC

I made my first visit to the Duke Infectious Diseases Clinic in October of 1992. Hyung Goo had recently been diagnosed with Kaposi's sarcoma, and he took me along to his regular meeting with his social worker so that we could all talk together about the implications of the diagnosis. I walked in the door, and encountered the social worker, a woman, dressed as a man, complete with fedora and penciled-on mustache. Nearby stood a male nurse dressed as a female nurse, in cap, tights, and dress. Vampires lurked in the background. It was Halloween. It was also an altogether fitting introduction to the ID clinic, where the craziness of HIV and AIDS were met, and to some small degree neutralized, by an intentional countercraziness borne of a recognition that this was, in fact, no normal disease, as modern Western medicine liked to think of normal.

John Bartlett was the director of the ID clinic. He had come to Duke from Harvard in 1981 as an intern in medicine. Among the patients he saw during his three years of residency were some with AIDS, and in 1984 he began a fellowship in infectious diseases. At that time, Duke was just setting up a new HIV clinic. John had planned to leave academic medicine for private practice, but when he was invited to join the staff of the ID clinic, he accepted. He saw it as an opportunity to do something out of the ordinary run of medical practice, an opportunity to make a unique contribution, rather than being one of many doctors doing much the same thing.

The experience was exhilarating, and exhausting, and socially isolating. Five people ran the clinic: John, three nurses,

52

and a pharmacist. As the only physician, John was on call every day. At first they had only a handful of patients, and very little idea how best to care for them. What should you do for a patient with a fever of 39° and 10 T-cells? Nobody knew. There was no practice paradigm for the treatment of AIDS. It was up to the clinic staff to figure it out. They talked, they tried one thing and another, they designed and participated in research protocol after research protocol. They had a great deal of independence in deciding how the clinic ran, and in developing strategies for understanding and treating the disease.

They were also not immune from the prejudice surrounding HIV and AIDS. John's friends teased him: Was he having a midlife crisis? Wouldn't it be simpler to take antidepressants? The initial stigma was related to the association of the disease with homosexuality. As the 1980s wore on, it became increasingly clear that this was an infectious disease, although the specific means of transmission were yet unknown. What the clinic staff called the "Mars mentality" descended in many clinical settings: gloves, gowns, masks, patient isolation. But John and the rest of his staff would already have had AIDS if it could be contracted by caregiving. Experience made them unafraid, and their willingness to respond to patients' longing for human touch gave them an edge in caring for them.

John's wife, Trish, was also a member of the clinic staff. After graduating with a B.A. from Duke, she had done a graduate degree in social work at Boston University. During her years in Boston, she had sung in a Gilbert and Sullivan group, where she met a Welsh patter baritone named Jeffrey. Eventually Trish moved back to North Carolina, and Jeffrey moved to New York City. They kept in touch, and in 1982 she found out he was sick with what was then called GRID—Gay-Related Immune Disease. All summer long, as Jeffrey fell ill with pneumonia, Kaposi's sarcoma, cytomegalovirus, toxoplasmosis, Trish flew to New York on weekends to help care for him. In the fall, his friends found themselves increasingly at odds with his doctors about what might constitute appropriate medical care. In December Jeffrey's friends took him out of the hospital against medical advice and flew him to Wales to be with his mother.

He died in January of 1983, a good death, in hospice care. Trish promised Jeffrey that, as she had opportunity, she would try to be part of providing humane care for other people in situations like his.

Trish joined the staff of the ID clinic in 1988, where one of her first projects was a program designed to coordinate and assess home care for people with AIDS. The clinic had been organized on an outpatient model, which represented a new approach to AIDS care in North Carolina. Many AIDS-related conditions had previously been treated only in the hospital. But many patients did not want to be in the hospital; they wanted to be at home, where their privacy could be preserved, and where they could have more control and receive more support. But there were enormous challenges in mobilizing infrastructure for home care. Patients were not concentrated in an urban area (as in San Francisco or New York), but diffused throughout the state. There was a great deal of prejudice; it was difficult to find home health nurses, and even harder to find doctors, who would care for people with AIDS. Most homecare agencies were unwilling even to consider supporting intravenous therapy or administering experimental medications at home. The exception was Biomedical Home Care, one of whose nurses, Sandy Hendrickson, was the first AIDS case manager in North Carolina. She played a major role in changing the status quo, traveling all over the state, doing AIDS education at home care agencies, talking with patients, addressing issues and solving problems no one else would touch, until her death with breast cancer in 1994.

Trish's job, when she first joined the clinic staff, was to see what progress had been made to that point. What services were available? Were patients satisfied? What was their quality of life? Unsurprisingly, the surveys found that most patients would much rather be treated on an outpatient basis when possible, and that home care was in many cases much less expensive than inpatient treatment. The surveys also showed that everyone, whether hospitalized or not, was profoundly depressed. Many patients had problems, like addictions, in addition to HIV and AIDS. Patients' families were distressed—

their child was sick, often gay, and they didn't know what to do. The clinic didn't see many married couples, but in those they did see, there was tremendous hostility. But when Trish would request therapy for a patient or family, the department of psychiatry would turn her down. Why waste time doing therapy with someone who is going to die? What difference could it make?

In 1989, psychiatry sent over four social work students who had expressed interest in working with people with AIDS. But the students came with demands. They wanted promises that they wouldn't be infected with HIV, that they wouldn't be exposed to tuberculosis, that they would be assigned only patients with "insight" (that is, the intellectual capacity to assess and work on problems). But the clinic's patients were prostitutes, gay and bisexual people who were angry, people who didn't know what the problems were, who had unchecked addictions and marital problems, who were ineligible for other support programs because they were dying. The students were not up for this. Patients who saw them didn't want to go back. Trish finally sent them all away.

In 1990, another social work student expressed an interest in working at the clinic. Martha Zimmerman had dropped out of college during the Vietnam War, and spent several years working as an airline stewardess. She was one of a crew of eight or ten who traveled with the White House press corps whenever they would charter a plane to accompany the president on overseas trips. Martha met her husband, a journalist, on one of these trips, at which point she quit being a stewardess but continued traveling. They lived for several years in Hong Kong, and in 1988 moved to Chapel Hill, North Carolina, where a year later Martha entered a graduate program in social work.

It took Trish some time to be willing to take a chance on Martha. Eventually she recognized that Martha was willing to look at a person with AIDS as a human being, not as a dead person. The most pressing issue in a patient's life might not be dying, but something else. Patients couldn't identify these problems for themselves; they needed a therapist to work with them to identify the issues. With this kind of support, they could be helped to better deaths, and to better relationships with their family members and caregivers.

Martha's presence in the clinic was a big change. To this point the physicians, of whom there were now several, had been providing all the therapy. Trish had been coordinating home care and making referrals. Martha added a new role. She supervised a variety of projects: a group of University of North Carolina law students drew up wills and powers of attorney for clinic patients; churches contributed money to pay for patients' health insurance, saving the hospital thousands of dollars a year in indigent patient care. But her primary function was as a therapist, providing individual therapy in the safety of the clinic setting, where patients could be assured they would be treated with empathy and respect. Martha ended up working at the clinic during both of the years of her graduate program at UNC, and when she graduated, in the spring of 1991, she joined the clinic staff as its second full-time social worker.

We knew none of this when, in the summer of 1991, we returned to Durham as newlyweds. Hyung Goo got a job at Duke Medical Center, and it seemed a natural thing for him to look for medical care at Duke as well. One day he went to the clinic for an initial appointment. He came home and reported that he had been assigned to a staff physician and set up on a regular routine of blood work and monthly preventive treatments for pneumonia. The physician had also observed that he seemed depressed, and had asked him if he wanted to talk with a social worker. She would meet with him on a regular basis, if he liked; there would be no charge. "Do they do this for everyone?" we wondered. At that time, they did. Once Martha was a member of the clinic staff, any patient who seemed to need therapeutic support was offered the opportunity to meet with her.

Martha became an enormously important person to Hyung Goo and to me. She commented to Hyung Goo, early in their relationship, that the experience of the serious illness and death of a spouse could be a very intimate one for both partners in a marriage. This helped to give us a vision for our life together: we had the opportunity to come closer and closer together in the midst of whatever happened. Even before I met her, she provided to both of us what was in essence marital counseling. On numerous occasions, Hyung Goo would come back from talking with Martha about some difficult issue, and as he sat at the dining-room table rehearsing the details of their conversation ("and I said to her . . . and then she said to me . . .") it was as if Martha herself were there with us, saying, "Yes, you two can deal with this together," taking some of the pressure off, being our coach and sometimes even our referee.

As significant as Martha became to me, she was incomparably more significant to Hyung Goo. He met with her nearly every week for the four years he was a patient at the clinic. As both his therapist and his caseworker, she accompanied him from when he was HIV-positive but still asymptomatic, through his official diagnosis with AIDS, worsening complications, huge adjustments in lifestyle and outlook, to his death. She helped him deal with insurance paperwork, Social Security, management of symptoms and medications, hospital and home health agency bureaucracies. She worked with him in addressing psychological and relational issues having to do with his illness: the fact that we could not have children, issues of confidentiality, depression and anxiety, the losses involved in leaving work and becoming sicker and sicker, his concerns about what would become of me after his death. They became deeply attached to one another, and when he died, she grieved for him as for a friend.

John Bartlett played an equally significant role in our lives. Hyung Goo was seen at first by one of the other clinic physicians, but after a year or two, she moved to another practice, and Hyung Goo was reassigned to John. John was a collaborative physician, one who strove to empower and accompany his patients. Where Hyung Goo was concerned, this collaboration took on particular depth and intensity. Like the scientist that he was, Hyung Goo was observant and analytical. He would go to John with lists of symptoms and questions, and they would sit and talk and try to figure it out. Partly because Hyung Goo worked so hard to manage his health, he lived to have a lot more complicated things wrong with him at once than many other AIDS patients did. By the end, he and John were working in the dark much of the time, trying to find their way through a combination of problems that even John had never encountered before. With typical generosity, John told me after Hyung Goo's death that Hyung Goo had been one of his best teachers. "He would come in with brilliant self-diagnoses, and interview me, and I would sit there and learn." In fact, Hyung Goo knew that John was a better doctor for having had Hyung Goo as a patient. It gave Hyung Goo a feeling of having contributed, in a small but still significant way, to the care of other persons with AIDS, and to medical science generally.

This much we were aware of during Hyung Goo's life. With the solipsism of illness, we didn't consider whether there had been a darker side to John's experience of caring for Hyung Goo. I realized only later what an exceptionally challenging patient Hyung Goo had been for all of the clinic doctors, and for John in particular. Hyung Goo had so much wrong with him, and no one knew what to do. And Hyung Goo could formulate so many questions that no one knew how to answer. The clinic doctors were always faced with questions they couldn't answer; that was part of treating patients with AIDS. But Hyung Goo could come up with brand-new questions, questions they had never thought of, that they couldn't answer. With no malicious intent at all, he rubbed their noses in the limits of their understanding. It was enormously frustrating. They wanted so much to fix it, and they couldn't.

If Martha and John were the fixed stars in our universe, the rest of the clinic staff revolved around us, and them. This, at least, was how we experienced it. At the time that Hyung Goo was there, the clinic had a patient load of about six hundred, with a staff of six doctors and a dozen other clinicians—nurses, aides, physician's assistants. At one time or another, Hyung Goo was cared for by all of them. During the periods when he was the most ill, we were in the clinic or on the phone with one or another of the staff almost every day. Most patients did not use the clinic this heavily. But we lived only five minutes away, and Hyung Goo took a very active interest in his health and in the management of his illness. The clinic staff responded to this, going out of their way for us time and again. One of the nurses once came to our house to draw Hyung Goo's blood, so he wouldn't have to go out in the summer heat. One of the nurses' aides made it her special mission to say to me, practically every time she laid eyes on me, "You're a good wife." Toward the end of Hyung Goo's life, it seemed as if the entire staff of the clinic did nothing but take care of us.

And they did so in a way that acknowledged and respected the special relationships that we had with John and Martha. In the summer of 1995, John was away from the clinic for several months, participating in a hospital-sponsored medical exchange program. Hyung Goo had been extremely ill the preceding spring, and we all knew it was more than possible that he would die sometime that summer. We were not happy that John was going away. I went in to the clinic with Hyung Goo to meet the physician who would look after him in John's absence. As our conversation with him drew to a close, Dr. Hicks said, "I know I'm not John, but I'll take the best care of you I can."

"Here is someone I can trust," I thought.

That fall, Hyung Goo was in the hospital, obviously dying. Martha's father was scheduled for elective surgery, and she had agreed to travel to his home and care for him for a week. Martha was as distraught as we at the prospect of her being out of town when Hyung Goo died. "I knew this would happen," she said, weeping. "I knew it."

The day she left, Trish came by Hyung Goo's hospital room. "I know I'm not Martha," she said to me, "but call me any time, with anything."

It seems incredible now that we should have been the recipients of such love and affection from a group of people who were, after all, busy professionals with hundreds of other patients to care for. It seems incredible that we should have had such free and open access to medical care at least as good as that available anywhere else in the world. It seems incredible that that care should have cost us virtually nothing out of pocket, as a result of the excellent insurance that Hyung Goo had as a Duke Medical Center employee.

It did happen, but it won't happen again. Too much has changed. AIDS has changed, and the clinic has changed with it. In 1995, the year of Hyung Goo's death, 21 percent of the total patient population of the clinic died, nearly one hundred and fifty deaths. The following year, there were seventy-six deaths, out of a larger total number of patients. What made the difference? Protease inhibitors, a powerful new class of medications that reduced viral load and improved both quality and quantity of life for significant numbers of patients. But protease inhibitors were no panacea; they brought with them at least as many problems as promises. They were complex to administer, difficult to tolerate, and fabulously expensive. And it was unclear just how long their effects on individual patients' lives would last. For months after their introduction, the clinic staff held their collective breath, waiting for all the patients who had shown initial improvement to crash at once.

At the same time, the demographics of the patient population were shifting. When the clinic first opened, most of its patients were gay and bisexual men of relatively high socio-economic and educational levels. By the late 1990s, the common theme was no longer homosexuality, but poverty. The clinic's patients included equal numbers of men and women; a majority were now black, with an increasing number of Hispanics. HIV was often the least of the patients' concerns. Getting sick was off in the future; they were more worried about where to live, how to eat, how to get drugs, both legal and illegal. Providing long-term care to persons with HIV and AIDS became more complex as patients started living longer and were poorer to begin with. Churches wanted to help, but patients were often suspicious, and had lots of habits that churches wished they didn't have. Black churches were slow to come around, even as AIDS and HIV became more significant problems in the black community.

And the sheer number of patients continued to increase. In 1990 the clinic had four or five hundred patients in all; in 1998 there were about eleven hundred patients. Part of the increase was due to new therapies that allowed patients to live longer; part of it was due to a rise in the absolute number of HIV-infected people. A "third wave" of HIV infection had begun to manifest itself. The first wave had been gay men and IV drug users. The second wave was the sexual partners of gay men and IV drug users. The third wave was people in rural areas, as the infection began to find its way there. The Southeast was the epicenter of this third wave. Unlike urban areas, where large amounts of money and education were available for treatment and prevention, little of either was available in the rural Southeast. In 1996, the North Carolina state legislature passed a law requiring public schools to promote abstinence until marriage; in response, many school systems dropped all sex education from their curricula, fearing that any conversation about sex would be contrary to state law. A few years later, the clinic was seeing more and more patients in their early twenties, people who had evidently been infected as teenagers, who had no idea how they had been exposed to HIV, or even that they were at risk.

These three factors—the introduction of protease inhibitors; a patient population that was less and less gay, white, and male, and increasingly poor, black, and female; and an ever-increasing total number of patients—both created and required significant changes in how the clinic went about its business. Protease inhibitors had such a significant effect on patients' lives that it seemed imperative to give as many patients as possible access to them, but they were so expensive that this was not easy. Patients without insurance could not possibly afford them; patients with insurance could quickly exceed their maximum lifetime coverage. The focus of the clinic's social workers began to shift from providing direct patient services to finding sources of funding for medication. As increasing numbers of patients came from utterly disenfranchised segments of society, the services the clinic did offer shifted from counseling to assistance with rent, food, transportation, child care. As patient life spans increased, the focus of treatment shifted from crisis management to a more longitudinal approach. And as the number of patients and the size of the staff increased, the clinic began to lose the intimacy and the intense relationships between patients and staff that had characterized it in the early years.

Thus as I look back on Hyung Goo's and my experience at the ID clinic, I feel that I am looking back, not just at a period in my own life that is past, but at a bygone era in the life of the clinic and in the story of AIDS in general. Hyung Goo died at the peak of the AIDS epidemic in the United States. The month he died, the clinic experienced the most patient deaths it had ever had in a single month. Within another month, the numbers had begun to go down, and have been declining steadily ever since. These statistics mirror those of the nation as a whole. The epidemic is far from over, but it has changed form. Things are not the way they used to be; and for many people living with HIV and AIDS, that is good news. But for me, there is a poignancy about the changes that have taken place since Hyung Goo's life and death. Of course we would have preferred that there had been better treatments available, that he had felt better and lived longer and been able to do more of the things he wanted to do. But what if "better treatment" had come at such a cost that his health insurance was depleted before he died? And what if longer life had had to be lived without the intensely personal medical care and therapeutic support that he found so healing in the final years of his life?

"No one ever gets to know what might have been," Aslan says to Lucy in *The Voyage of the Dawn Treader*. She had behaved badly and wished she knew the good that might have been. I am thankful I know the good that was. A clinic staff who began as medical caregivers became as family to us: a community of people upon whom we knew we could depend to care for us gladly and generously, not just as professionals but as fellow human beings. We were grateful for their technical expertise, and even more grateful for their compassion. "It's really changed us," Trish said to me, speaking of her and others' work in the clinic. It changed me, too. It is not possible thus to be served in the midst of illness and pain and fear and loss, and not be changed.

# ASCENDING

Early in Hyung Goo's and my marriage, I had a recurrent waking vision. We were walking together up an alpine mountainside, surrounded by grass and flowers and brilliant sunshine and breathtakingly beautiful scenery, but also by billowing clouds round about us that blocked off view of the summit.

As time went on, the clouds became grayer, the sun was not so often visible, the air became damper and cooler. The terrain became rockier and steeper, and the distance we could see ahead of us was reduced to a few steps. It was still an indescribably beautiful place to be, but the weather was changing.

# OCTOBER 8, 1992:
# KS DIAGNOSIS

A diagnosis of AIDS comes in two parts: a positive test for antibodies to HIV, and the presence of one or more "AIDS-defining
conditions," that is, infections or tumors indicating a compromised immune system. For the person who has tested positive
for HIV before becoming ill, the diagnosis of an AIDS-defining
condition is equivalent to a diagnosis of AIDS. It marks the
transition from being HIV-positive but asymptomatic to having
AIDS. The list of AIDS-defining conditions has evolved over the
years, as AIDS itself has evolved and spread from one sector
of the population to another. Early AIDS-defining conditions
were those most typically seen in gay men, like tuberculosis and
thrush and certain kinds of pneumonia; as AIDS has become
an illness more prevalent among women, AIDS-defining conditions have come to include things like cervical cancer and
yeast infections.

The list of AIDS-defining conditions was in flux in 1992.
Early in the year, the Centers for Disease Control announced
that, beginning in January of 1993, a T-cell count below 200,
together with a positive HIV-antibody test, would qualify as
a diagnosis of AIDS, even in the absence of acute illness. In
May of 1992, Hyung Goo's T-cell count fell below 200. Did he
have AIDS, or not? Yes and no, we found ourselves saying to
ourselves and to those very few people who knew of Hyung
Goo's HIV infection. He didn't have AIDS officially, since the
change in definition wouldn't go into effect until the following

January; but given that in eight months his present condition would be described as AIDS, it seemed that for all practical purposes, he did already have it.

In October of 1992, Hyung Goo was diagnosed with Kaposi's sarcoma. That put an end to his in-between status with respect to AIDS. Kaposi's sarcoma was one of the most venerable of AIDS-defining conditions. It was a kind of tumor of the capillaries that showed up as purple blotches on the skin, and had been quite uncommon until it was observed in several young gay men in New York City who were also suffering from various other immune-related disorders. The presence of KS in these patients raised the question whether their illnesses were somehow related, and played a role in the characterization of AIDS as an illness in its own right.

And now Hyung Goo had KS, and along with it, an official diagnosis of AIDS. In a sense, KS was the best way to receive an AIDS diagnosis. Most AIDS-defining conditions were debilitating illnesses in themselves. KS was just purple spots. It wasn't painful; it wasn't malignant. The spots just appeared here and there—a few on his face, a few on his arm, a few on his leg. It was more something to worry about than something to do anything about. Dutifully, we worried. What if people could tell Hyung Goo had AIDS just from seeing his KS lesions? That turned out not to be worth worrying about. No one recognized a KS lesion on sight, not even physicians who knew that Hyung Goo had AIDS. In the emergency room, once, the resident pointed to a spot and said, "What is this little hematoma?"

"That's Kaposi's sarcoma," we said.

"Oh," she said.

Hyung Goo worried that he would develop so many KS lesions that he would be truly disfigured. This fear was a little more realistic. Some people did develop a great deal of KS; in the transfusion room at Beth Israel Hospital we saw a man who was purple from head to foot. What if this happened to Hyung Goo? Would he look so bad by the time he died that the casket couldn't be open for viewing? The undertaker assured us that they could fix him up just fine. As it happened, Hyung Goo's KS lesions remained relatively few and relatively small, but either the undertaker remembered our conversation or else he just had an aversion to purple spots. When I looked at Hyung Goo's body as it had been prepared for viewing, I discovered that they had covered his face with pancake makeup. He looked like he was ready for display at Madame Tussaud's. I made them wipe it all off.

The real significance of KS, for us, was not medical; it was symbolic and practical. Hyung Goo didn't feel any more ill after it had been diagnosed than before, but afterwards he had AIDS, whereas he hadn't before. We had been living so long in dreadful anticipation of the day when Hyung Goo would have AIDS—he since he had tested HIV-positive nearly eight years earlier; I since he had told me of his HIV infection three years earlier. Now the day was finally here.

The diagnosis came midweek. That weekend, we attended a conference on modern English hymnody. The presentations were thought-provoking; the music was beautiful; even the weather was lovely. We had a wonderful time. It seemed incongruous—how could we have such a good time in the wake of such bad news? It didn't seem odd to Martha, who had seen something similar in other people with AIDS. The diagnosis of the first AIDS-defining condition brought with it a kind of relief: after years of wondering how the diagnosis would come, now we knew, and the energy that had been consumed in worrying about possible scenarios could be redirected toward living in the midst of what had actually happened.

The practical effect of Hyung Goo's KS diagnosis was that we decided to tell our families that Hyung Goo had AIDS. At the time that Hyung Goo had first tested positive for HIV, he had told very few people, and no one in his family except one cousin. He was too shocked, and too ashamed, and too terrified, to do anything except withdraw from virtually all relationships and wait to die. As the years passed and he didn't die, he began to reconnect with people and with life, but he still kept his HIV status very private. He didn't care to lose his job or his insurance, and he was particularly worried about rejection where his family was concerned. The stigma against homosexuality is, if anything, greater in Asian societies than in the West. Even if he didn't disclose any details of how he had become infected, AIDS itself carried that stigma, and Hyung Goo feared that it would be more than his family was prepared to deal with.

When we became engaged, we debated whether we should tell our families about Hyung Goo's HIV infection. It was such a material consideration in our decision to marry that we felt we really were concealing something from them if we said nothing about it. On the other hand, what would be the point of telling them? My family barely knew Hyung Goo. Wouldn't it be easier for them to welcome him as a new member of the family if we held off telling them about his HIV status until later? And Hyung Goo's family had experienced several crises in the previous year or two. Would being told of Hyung Goo's HIV status be too crushing an emotional blow? We didn't feel we could tell either family without telling both, and in the end we told neither. We were truly happy to be getting married, and we wanted our families to be happy, too. We wanted them to come to our wedding and rejoice, and we knew that if we told them that Hyung Goo had HIV, they would come to our wedding and weep. We decided that Hyung Goo's HIV status was no one's business but ours, and said nothing.

But now Hyung Goo had AIDS. As much as we had hoped this moment would be a long time in coming, it was here now. It seemed that a clock had started to tick. At that time, the early 1990s, people typically lived about eighteen months after an AIDS diagnosis. We couldn't bring ourselves to believe that time was really that short, but we felt our horizons closing in. Did we want to wait to tell our families until Hyung Goo was critically ill? Or did we want to tell them now, while he was still in relatively good health, and while there was still time and energy for conversation, and for reconciliation and healing in relationships that were broken or distant? We decided to tell them now.

But how to do it? We lived at a distance from both families— mine was in Iowa, Hyung Goo's was in Boston, and we were in North Carolina. Hyung Goo felt strongly that the news should be broken in a face-to-face meeting rather than a telephone call

67

or a letter, but opportunities for such meetings were limited. We had plans to see both families over the holidays, but was it really fair to drop the AIDS bomb on everyone over Christmas? And there was an additional problem with Christmas. Those visits would be only a few days long. Would there be enough time to process so significant a piece of news? Or would the effect be akin to lobbing a hand grenade into a crowd and then going home, leaving everyone else to pick up the pieces? Perhaps, if we chose to tell them over the holidays, it would be better to give some advance notice of what was coming, and use the time together for conversation rather than for disclosure.

And what should we say? Should we volunteer any details of how Hyung Goo had become infected? People would certainly wonder. Should we satisfy their curiosity, or should we simply tell them of his AIDS diagnosis and leave the rest to their imaginations? I felt a certain obligation to pony up information about how Hyung Goo had become infected; Hyung Goo thought it was irrelevant to the present situation, and nobody's business anyway.

And then there was the issue of timing. I was getting ready to take my comprehensive exams for my doctoral program. I had finished my two years of coursework, and was busy studying for a series of examinations, both written and oral, that I had to pass in order to proceed to the dissertation-writing stage of my program. The written exams were scheduled over the first two weeks of December, with the oral exam at the end of the second week. The last thing I needed was for a family conflagration about Hyung Goo and AIDS to erupt in the middle of my exam preparation. Whatever we did, we couldn't do it until my exams were over.

After hours of conversation with Martha, we had a plan. We would write a letter to our families, telling them that we had something important to discuss with them over the holidays, and we wanted them to know in advance what it was. We would tell them that Hyung Goo had recently received a diagnosis of AIDS after having been HIV-positive but asymptomatic for eight years, but we would not disclose any other background information. We would offer general reassurances about the state of his health, and about my health, and invite them to call us if they wanted to talk before seeing us at Christmas or New Year's. We would wait until I had taken my final written exam, and would then mail a copy of the letter to each member of our immediate families. The letter would presumably not arrive at any of its destinations until after my oral exam was over, but, just to be sure, we wouldn't answer the telephone until then.

We wrote the letter. I took my exams. We mailed the letter. I sat for my oral. I passed, having successfully managed to convey to the examining committee the false impression that I had my mind fully on the details of the exegesis and theology of Luther and Calvin, Wesley and Barth, Anselm and Athanasius. And we waited for the phone to ring. It didn't take long. Virtually everyone to whom we had sent the letter called us within hours of receiving it. They were stunned, saddened, nearly speechless. We didn't know what to say, either.

A week later, we gathered with my family for Christmas. No one mentioned the letter. Hyung Goo and I huddled in the kitchen, so stressed we could barely function. Should we bring the subject up? Let them bring it up, we decided. If they didn't want to talk about it, we wouldn't talk about it. Perhaps they were waiting for us to take the lead. In any case, nothing had been said by anyone by the time we left. The next week we were in Boston with Hyung Goo's family. They did talk about it—not much, but enough to say how sorry they were, and that they loved us. Hyung Goo remembered his fears of rejection and condemnation, and felt a little ashamed of not having expected better from them all along.

Hyung Goo's sister told me, several months after his death, that the family had loved Hyung Goo but had often not known *how* to love him. We saw something akin to this in both our families' reactions to the news of Hyung Goo's AIDS diagnosis. They felt very badly for us, they wanted to be supportive, and they had no idea what to do. As the next few years progressed, both families helped us financially. My parents sent us a check every month; Hyung Goo's aunts and uncles gave us cash every time they saw us, or so it seemed. But no one ever knew what to say, and we—being, after all, members of these same fami-

69

lies—didn't know how to open the door to conversation with them.

And yet, that diagnosis of Kaposi's sarcoma, and our subsequent decision to tell our families that Hyung Goo had AIDS, marked the beginning of the end of our self-imposed isolation from nearly everyone we knew in relation to Hyung Goo's illness. Gradually our public and private selves came together, as we told our families, then a few friends, and a few more, and a few more, until we had abandoned any effort to control who knew and who didn't. And as we did so, we took our place in the world of AIDS, no longer trying to give the impression to anyone that that was not our world, but rather acknowledging to everyone, ourselves included, that this was where we lived.

# BODIES IN THE WATER

One beautiful spring morning in 1993, I was standing at the entrance to the Duke Divinity School library, talking with two of my fellow graduate students about psychotherapy. I talked regularly with Mark about my therapy, which I had begun about a year before, and Lucas was himself seeing a therapist. Lucas told us a story of a dream he had had, in which he had been lying on a beach, his head on his therapist's stomach, the waves lapping gently at the shore. He had found the imagery of this dream slightly alarming,  and had asked his therapist whether she thought this was a particularly weird or worrisome dream. Oh, no, she had said. It was a very positive dream. She would only have been worried if the dream had been scary, or if the waves had been violent.

"Oh, Lucas," I said. "I don't even want to know what your therapist would make of my dreams." And I told them about a dream I had had recently, in which I had been running, terrified, through a large and labyrinthine building, pursued by a bad guy. In my dream, I emerged from the building onto a long, rickety dock that was high above the water, swaying back and forth in a violent storm, threatening to collapse at any moment. I was leaning over a railing, looking at dead bodies floating in the water, and vomiting over and over and over again into the water below.

"I really don't think you should let your therapist do this to you," Mark said, looking pale. But I had figured out enough about therapy at that point to know that the therapist wasn't doing this to me. This dream was me. Could I bear to face it, to face myself?

# DREAMING
# WITH SALVADOR DALI

The only reason I ever went to see a therapist was because Hyung Goo was sick. I was anxious about him, and he was worried about me. "You really should find someone to talk to," he said. Finally, I did. Martha referred me to a social work intern at the Duke Psychiatric Outpatient Clinic, who in turn referred me to a therapist in the community. Dan Grandstaff was a graduate of Princeton Theological Seminary. He had been in the pastoral ministry for some fifteen years before returning to graduate school in social work in Chapel Hill, North Carolina. He had been in private practice in Durham for a year or two when I started to see him in the summer of 1992.

"I just want to feel better," I announced to Dan at my initial interview. "I don't want to spend all kinds of time talking about my mother or my childhood or anything else."

"I'm not sure that will be possible," he said.

Sessions consisted largely of me glaring at Dan, and him looking placidly back at me. When I did have something to say, it was usually about my mother or my childhood. The entire exercise seemed idiotic, doubly so because within weeks I did, in fact, feel better. What was going on in those fifty-minute sessions, during which I felt stifled, irate, and contemptuous, and after which I could scarcely decide whether to faint or throw up, that could possibly make me feel better the rest of the week? I decided to quit.

73

But Hyung Goo was diagnosed with KS in October of 1992, and the stress associated with his AIDS diagnosis and the process of telling our families gave me a reason to continue seeing Dan. In January or February, Dan said, "Now that you're starting to open up a little more, perhaps we could talk about some of your dreams."

"I don't dream," I said.

"Well, if you ever did," he said.

I went home and dreamt. I dreamt and dreamt and dreamt, night after night, in vivid color, about boats and water and drowning, about cars and crowds of children, about skies full of stars in the middle of the day and hedges covered with big purple flowers like magnolias, about seals on broccoli lawns and crocodiles that got up and scuttled off like pantomime horses. I was up three and four times a night writing down my dreams. Some of them were pages long. "Does everyone dream like this?" I asked Dan.

"No," he said. "You have a gift." And he laughed.

I hated him. I hated his expressions of sympathy with my life, and with my experience of therapy. I hated the way he sat there, refusing to take the lead, waiting for me to say something, anything. I hated the way I seemed to lose my adult self the minute I walked into his office, becoming instead the miserable and furious child I used to be. And I hated my growing sense that I was there, in his office, not because of Hyung Goo's illness, as if this were my punishment for having married someone who was sick, but because I needed to be there for myself.

"Do you remember," I asked Dan in a letter I wrote to him, "in *Pilgrim's Progress,* how Christian falls asleep beside the way and loses his scroll, and goes on without it, and then when the lions menace him he is terrified, and realizes he hasn't got it, and has to make the miserable journey back to search for what he has lost? Well, I feel like I've gotten this far, and have only just realized that I've lost something vital, and I have to go back and find it before I can go on. The beasts that are snarling on every side are too ferocious to face without it; but unlike Christian, who at least knew what it was he'd lost, and where he'd last seen it, I don't know what I'm looking for or where

74

to find it. And my guide, the person whose hand I'm supposed to hold as I stumble back along the path in the darkness, is a man I don't know and can't stand.

"And so I'm furious with you. This damned path is so uneven, and I keep tripping and falling over things, and I think I've barked my shins a zillion times, and you just keep saying, 'Gee, I'm so sorry, but this is just the way it is.' Well, I don't like it. And I'm sure it's just going to get worse. It's not going to be very long before I move from just tripping over things to falling headlong into giant mud puddles, and then the shock and the nastiness of it will be such that I really won't be able to keep from bursting into tears, and I'll be sitting there weeping, covered with filth, and there you'll be: 'Gee, I'm so sorry.' Well, to hell with you and your sorryness. I'd rather be furious than pitiable, and I'd rather dig in my heels and refuse to go anywhere than be dragged into God-knows-where by you."

Toward the end of the spring, I had another opportunity to quit. My insurance would pay for forty weeks a year of therapy, and the fortieth week was coming up. I couldn't afford to pay Dan's full fee, so I told him I'd have to take a break. Maybe once the insurance kicked in again, I'd come back. Dan had another idea. I related it to my friend Mark over lunch. "He's willing to see you for only your copayment, without any insurance reimbursement?" Mark asked.

"Right," I said.

"Bastard!" Mark said.

I saw Dan for six years. As I came to understand that first year, there are two big psychotherapeutic questions: "How can I cope?" and "Who am I?" The first question is perhaps the more obvious one, since no one gets into therapy who isn't having trouble coping in one way or another. But the questions are related, because you can't cope except out of who you are. If you don't know who you are, you're going to have to find out. And if the energy you need for coping is tied up in unexpressed or unacknowledged sorrow or anger, then you have to figure that out and do something about it before you can redirect those resources toward the crises of the moment.

Not every challenge requires a full-scale renovation of the psyche. In this sense, therapy is like housecleaning—you can do a little of it or a lot, depending on what the situation requires. If the house isn't very dirty, maybe you can get by with a quick swipe at the sink. If all the company you're expecting is your next-door neighbor for a cup of coffee, you can push the unfolded laundry to one end of the couch and ignore it. But what if the house has never been cleaned? And what if your daughter has just announced that she'd like to have her wedding reception at home? A little straightening up is not going to be enough. You're going to need to strip the place to the walls, fix all the cracked plaster, send everything out to be cleaned, hold a couple of garage sales, and maybe paint the exterior and relandscape the yard while you're at it.

My experience of therapy was like this latter scenario. Hyung Goo and I had a very big event planned: we were going to accompany one another to his death. I had extremely limited psychological resources available to meet that challenge. If the self is like a house, I had been camped in the front hall all my life. Half of the doors leading to other rooms in the house were locked tight; the other half had been papered over so many years ago I'd forgotten they were there. Even the front hall wasn't very habitable, filled as it was with piles of jumbled-together stuff that I tripped over every time I turned around. I could barely maneuver even in the parts of myself with which I was familiar, and I was less-than-blissfully ignorant of what turned out to be vast reaches of my psyche.

As with housecleaning, things got worse before they got better. An old mess is often at least a familiar mess; when you start moving things around so you can really see what you're dealing with, it can seem that relative order has been replaced with chaos. And when I started to dream, it became apparent that there was unimaginably more to the house than just the front hall. Doors that I thought were tidily shut and locked were in fact straining at their hinges, ready to burst open at any moment from the pressure of whatever was on the other side of them. All my life I had been expending enormous amounts of energy trying to keep those doors closed. Now I needed that energy for other things.

I would have preferred to invest in new and better locks. Unfortunately, none seemed to be available. The only thing to do was to open the doors, be engulfed by the flood, and hope to survive. One by one, Dan and I located the doors, opened them up (or broke them down), and sorted through the mess inside: my relationship with my parents, my sense of myself as a woman and as a human being, decades-old anger and hurt and fear and confusion. Every time a door came crashing down, I felt like I was coming apart into a million tiny pieces that could never all be located again, much less put back together. Every time a room got even a little bit tidied up, I felt giddy with relief, free and spacious, like I had to keep taking deep breaths just to fill up all the space I had inside. And every time I got to such a point, I wanted to quit, like the person who has just survived a roller-coaster ride wants to get off. There was real exhilaration in making progress, but it didn't outweigh the sheer terror required to make it. But I couldn't get off; I couldn't stop, because Hyung Goo hadn't stopped being sick. On the contrary, he got sicker and sicker, so that no matter how much progress I made, I was always just barely keeping up with the demands of my life.

I didn't really begin to see the magnitude of the change that therapy had wrought in me until after Hyung Goo died. I had by then spent several years fighting on the border of my conscious and subconscious experience, furious that the distinction even existed, furious that its existence had been brought to my attention, terrified every time my inner life intruded into my conscious awareness (as in my dreams), terrified every time I found myself required consciously to attend to things of which I was seldom aware (as in therapy). When Hyung Goo died, it was as if that border, and the skirmishes associated with it, had ceased to exist. For the first six or nine months after his death, I experienced hardly any distinction at all between sleep and waking, dreaming and not dreaming, crying and not crying; it was all more or less the same, and I bobbed up and down in the midst of it all like a boat in the midst of a foggy sea. I wasn't

77

struggling any more. I wasn't angry; I wasn't frightened. I was just there, completely exhausted, awash with grief, buoyed by the knowledge that Hyung Goo and I had succeeded beyond all imagining in loving one another well.

Hyung Goo died in September. The following summer, I drove to Boston to attend my sister's wedding, visiting friends along the way there and back. I had taken several other trips since Hyung Goo's death, all of them fraught with exhaustion and emotion. This trip was different. I had all the driving to do myself, of course, but I felt up to it. I had dozens of people to see, but I felt up to that, too. I got tired; but when I was tired, I just felt tired, not undone. I felt open, alive, self-possessed, observant, receptive. It seemed that the entire quality of my experience was different from anything it had ever been before. The difference, I realized, was that I had never before had a functioning personality and no gigantic catastrophe to nego- tiate. Hyung Goo's and my marriage had been good for me, and therapy had been good for me, but all my gains in health and functioning were always diverted into dealing with Hyung Goo's illness. Like taxes, they got taken off the top, and we never saw them. But Hyung Goo was now no longer dying, and I was no longer in the midst of the worst of the grief of losing him; and for the first time, I could really begin to experience how much more whole I was than I had ever been before.

How much of the healing I experienced in those years was due to therapy? How much was due to marriage? I'll never know. It can't be sorted out. Hyung Goo, his illness, and our marriage created both the necessity and the possibility of ther- apy for me. Without his illness, I wouldn't have been stressed enough to seek therapy. Without our marriage, I wouldn't have had the safe haven I needed in order to face it. But without Dan, and his patient gift of years of time, attention, and expertise, I could never have entered into as deep and transformative an intimacy with Hyung Goo as I did. And without Dan, I would never have ventured forth from the illusory security of my crabbed and cramped sense of self into the startling, unpredictable, infinitely complex interior world of whose existence I had hitherto had absolutely no idea.

It is hard for me really to remember what my life was like before my experiences of marriage and of therapy. Perhaps Martha said it best. A couple of years after Hyung Goo died, we were reminiscing. She offered the opinion that there was no rational accounting for my decision to marry him: "No offense, Margaret, but you were really screwed up then."

# SEPTEMBER 30, 1993:
# LEAVING WORK

Not long after he had taken disability leave from his job, Hyung Goo introduced himself to a new acquaintance as a "retired molecular biologist." "I'd never met a retired molecular biologist before," Rich told me later. "The field is only ten or fifteen years old, and everyone in it is young; none of them has had a chance to retire."

Hyung Goo had become a molecular biologist by default. He gave up plans to attend medical school when he tested HIV-positive in his last year of undergraduate study, and took a job in cancer biology research at Massachusetts General Hospital instead. He worked for several years on a project that began with a specific genetic abnormality found in a tumor of the parathyroid gland and ended with the discovery of a gene that was involved in regulating the growth of all normal cells. As Hyung Goo put it, "I got published, and my boss got tenure."

But there wasn't anywhere for Hyung Goo to go from there. He couldn't rise through the ranks, moving from carrying out experiments (a lab tech's job) to designing experiments (a lab director's job), because to direct a lab it isn't enough to show yourself smart and capable; you have to have a Ph.D. or an M.D. So he stayed a lab tech, teaching molecular biology techniques to the steady stream of medical and doctoral students who passed through his lab on their research rotations, and watching them go on to direct their own labs while he stayed where he was.

When we got married, Hyung Goo took a job in a lab at Duke University Medical Center. Like the position he had had at Mass. General, the job was in cellular oncogenesis, investigating the workings of a gene involved in cell growth regulation. And like the job at Mass. General, it involved carrying out complex experiments aimed at answering questions that were very interesting but that had been posed by someone else.

Given the frustrations that were a constant accompaniment of his work, I thought it should be easy for Hyung Goo to leave his job when eventually he became too sick to work. It wasn't. Retirement is a complex transition even for a person who has reached a traditional retirement age, has compiled a satisfying record of achievement in his or her profession, and is in good enough health to be able to make happy plans for the future. When Hyung Goo retired, he was thirty-five, he had spent his entire working life in jobs that offered no opportunity for professional advancement, and he was terminally ill. The process of leaving his job was not just complex, it was agonizing.

Under the terms of his disability insurance, Hyung Goo could have left his job when he was diagnosed with Kaposi's sarcoma, and thus with AIDS, in the fall of 1992. But he felt well enough, and continued to work. The next spring, his health was worse, but not catastrophically so. He had a few more KS lesions, and a depressed white cell count for which he gave himself injections three times a week of a very expensive drug that made him feel crummy. His T-cell count fell below 100. I wrote to a friend, "Hyung Goo has lost 100 T-cells a year for the past three years. We're wondering if this means that in another year he'll have none; and, if so, if that means he'll be dead." He was exhausted all the time. He kept working.

At the beginning of the summer, I started driving him to work, so that he wouldn't have to walk the half mile to the lab in the stifling heat. By the end of the summer, I was driving him not because he preferred not to walk in the heat, but because he was too weak to do so. His exhaustion was compounded by the depression that had been a problem since long before HIV or AIDS was part of the picture. He slept poorly, was unable to get up in the morning, went into work in the early afternoon,

81

came home for dinner totally starved at 7 or 8, and then went back to work until the middle of the night.

It seemed obvious to me that Hyung Goo was not going to be able to keep this up much longer. It was less obvious to Hyung Goo. He didn't want to believe that his physical strength was diminishing. Work became a symbol of health: as long as he was working, he reasoned, he couldn't be too badly off. The longer he worked, and the tireder he got, the more I worried and fussed and urged him to quit. Each of us felt the other was being utterly unreasonable. He thought I was treating him as if he were more sick than he really was. I thought he was pushing himself ridiculously hard for no reason. Tensions rose; tempers flared. I was angry with everyone and everything, all of the time.

Dan would have been happy to be supportive, but I was too angry with him to take any comfort in talking to him. I went in to the clinic to talk to Martha. I sat in her office and cried and cried, and felt much better afterwards. She knew Hyung Goo so well. I didn't have to try to communicate to her what he was like; she knew already. She could see things in him that I, in the paradoxical self-absorption of anxiety, had so far failed to see. "Hyung Goo is very frightened," she said. Oh. I'd thought I was the one who was justifiably worried, and he was just being perverse.

Finally, Hyung Goo set a date to leave his job: September 30. Then his doctor found a patch of thrush in his mouth. Hyung Goo came home and announced that he would keep working, after all. He would also join several choral groups at Duke. His rationale? The thrush, if it got worse, might make it impossible for him to sing. If he wanted to sing, he had better do so now; but in case he had to give up singing, he had to keep working.

"Are you out of your mind?" I exploded. "What kind of fantasyland are you living in, that you think you can go from a full day's work to a two- or three-hour choral rehearsal, when your current pattern after a day's work is to be too tired even to eat? And if your thrush gets worse, I'm going to blame it on your refusal to adapt your schedule so you can get enough rest and preserve what health you have left."

"And what if my decision is to keep working until I drop dead?" Hyung Goo wanted to know.

Was work all that mattered to Hyung Goo? He appeared willing to sacrifice everything else—me, music, health, life—on that altar. I found this bizarre. It seemed utterly at odds with everything else he had ever said or done. I said as much, and more, to him, in heated tones. Hyung Goo made no response. He spent the rest of the day staring past me, refusing to talk or eat or respond in any way to anything.

I went to bed and dreamt, about cars and driving and road-blocks and bad guys. The bad guys surrounded our car; they raised the hood and started taking away pieces of the car. I cowered in the passenger seat, telling Hyung Goo to get us out of here before it was too late. Then suddenly he was no longer in the car; he was on the outside, looking in. I looked at him for some clue as to what to do, but received none, and woke up in a cold sweat.

"That dream seems pretty transparent," I wrote to Dan. "At least the end part does, where Hyung Goo is now out where the bad guys are, and I am inside by myself. I feel afraid—afraid that I am really starting to lose Hyung Goo. He said to me once, 'Don't you think that the day I stop working, I will start to die?' Maybe he's right. Maybe he will. I rebel against the very idea. It seems so needless. Why does he have to die when he stops working? Why can't he think of it not as losing, not as giving up, but as moving on? I don't know. He refuses to talk about it. And I feel abandoned, rejected, dismissed—not out of necessity, but by his choice. He simply doesn't want my company, and refuses to give me his."

A few days later, I talked to Martha again. "When Hyung Goo is acting so rejecting, do you feel he doesn't love you any more?" she asked.

A new understanding of what had been going on began to dawn on me. I was well aware that there were many people who, upon learning that I had married Hyung Goo in the knowledge that he was HIV-positive, thought, "Oh, isn't she brave." But it seemed to me that Hyung Goo was the brave one. How much courage must it have taken for him to ask me to marry him, knowing that he would become needy and dependent and disabled by illness, and yet believing himself to be a good potential partner for me nonetheless? I experienced his love for me as an expression of that courage. And when the inclination to isolate and reject overcame him, it seemed not that he had ceased to love, but that his courage was failing him.

Hyung Goo did leave his job on September 30. His doctor documented his need for disability leave in a letter stating that due to AIDS and progressive Kaposi's sarcoma, Hyung Goo was completely and permanently disabled; his prognosis was very poor and he was not expected ever to be able to return to work. "A scary letter," Hyung Goo called it. The arguments we had had with one another toward the end of the summer played a significant role in his finally making the transition to retirement, but neither of us wanted to make any more transitions that way. Martha coached us. "Back off sooner," she said to me. It was good advice. At the very least, I felt less rejected, and he felt less like I wouldn't leave him alone. And as I learned not to demand too much of Hyung Goo when he was feeling sick or upset, he came to realize that a quiet word or two from him could offer real comfort to me, comfort that he became ever quicker to offer even—or especially—when he felt unwell.

A consequence of Hyung Goo's retirement was that we began to allow the fact that Hyung Goo had AIDS to become common knowledge. We had told our families the previous Christmas, and had told some of our friends in Boston since then. But virtually no one in Durham knew, and Hyung Goo preferred to keep it that way. As long as he was working, it wasn't a difficult secret to keep. But once he retired, routine questions about work had either to be deflected or to be answered with outright lies. Hyung Goo found deflection, supplemented with untruths as needed, the path of least resistance—it was easier than telling people he had AIDS and having to deal with their emotional response. But I hated having to be evasive or make up stories to cover up the fact that Hyung Goo wasn't working. It was stressful to try to think of plausible falsehoods. It was easier just to tell the truth; and if people got upset, that was their problem.

We had imagined that once we stopped being very selective about whom we told and binding them to secrecy the news would rapidly make its way through the grapevine and everyone would know. It didn't happen. To judge from the number of people we had to tell ourselves, virtually everyone treated the disclosure as a personal confidence and didn't discuss it with anyone else. We appreciated not being the subjects of gossip, but it did mean that we were faced over and over with people who didn't know and had to be told. Eventually we developed a system for breaking the news that satisfied both Hyung Goo's desire not to upset people, and my desire to be straightforward. When we met someone new, or when we realized that a prior acquaintance still didn't know, I would take the person aside and tell him or her privately. Then I would tell Hyung Goo that I'd told whomever it was. Then we would all know that we all knew, and we could proceed from there.

A longer-term result of Hyung Goo's retirement from his job was that he eventually had time and energy for some of the other things he enjoyed. The first few months after he left his job, he was too tired and depressed to do much of anything. In January and February, he became seriously ill with an eye infection and then with pneumonia. Those bouts of illness made plain beyond the shadow of a doubt that he could not possibly have continued to work, and perhaps gave him greater freedom to embrace his retirement. That summer, we spent two months in Boston, visiting with friends and family. Hyung Goo began playing his violin again. In the fall, we were back in Durham. Hyung Goo audited classes in music theory and in German; he sang in an early-music ensemble; he wrote a memoir.

In the end, however, the most significant consequence of Hyung Goo's retirement was that he was able to devote himself more fully to what came to seem his life's work, namely me. On one of our first dates, Hyung Goo told me that if he had to choose between professional success and being a good husband and family man, he would choose the latter. I had no idea at the time how poignant this statement was, coming as it did from a man who had practically no hope of ever having either a substantive career or a family. As it turned out, he did have a family: he had me. And he devoted himself to me with a passionate, reflective, quirky intensity that transformed me from deep within, as I found myself received and nurtured and delighted in as I had never been before.

A few months after Hyung Goo's death, I had lunch in Boston with one of Hyung Goo's friends from the chorus. Rini had first met me when Hyung Goo and I were dating. She recalled me as quiet and shy, "like a perfect little rosebud," with everything just so, and shut tight, all closed up. But in the years since then, I'd been opening up, a petal here and a petal there, and then more and more, with petals all over the place, to the point that it was impossible that I should ever get closed up again. I had to laugh at this image of a rose gone completely berserk. "It was Hyung Goo's doing," I said.

"Yes," said Rini. "It was his gift to you."

# SING ME TO HEAVEN

Hyung Goo and I had dinner one evening with a group of musicians who were mostly strangers to us. Hyung Goo was seated at the end of the table, next to a distinguished violist. The violist was a quiet and shy man, but before long Hyung Goo had engaged him in a conversation about the viola and the viola repertoire. The violist mentioned the Schnittke viola concerto, a work then so new that it had only recently been premiered in the United States. "Are you familiar with the work?" the violist asked.

"I've heard it three times!" Hyung Goo said.

The Schnittke concerto had received its U.S. premiere in Boston, in a series of performances by the Russian violist Yuri Bashmet. The program had also included the Verdi *Te Deum*, in which Hyung Goo had sung as a member of the Tanglewood Festival Chorus. Each evening, before the Verdi was performed, Hyung Goo had gone upstairs to the balcony and sat in the back to hear the first half of the program. Hyung Goo and the distinguished violist spent the rest of the evening absorbed in discussion of the Schnittke concerto and Bashmet's performance of it.

We left the dinner before the violist did. We heard the next day that after we had gone, the violist turned to another guest and said, "Who was that young man?"

Hyung Goo was a "musician's musician," as a friend of ours once said to me. By this he meant, I think, that Hyung Goo combined a passionate love of music and an encyclopedic knowl-

87

edge of the subject with an ability to engage other musicians in intelligent and interesting conversation about any musical topic whatever.

I was a musician, too, or I had been when I was in college. Hyung Goo had first decided to ask me out in part because he judged that my love of music might be comparable to his own. In fact, I possessed nothing like the musical sensitivity and knowledge that he did; but I did love music, and I loved Hyung Goo as a musician, and the way that a life with him was inevitably a life filled with music and musicians and music-making.

Hyung Goo had begun to learn to play the violin in the sixth grade. His teachers, all public-school employees, ranged over the years from a band director who played the trumpet and knew nothing about the violin, to an Armenian from Puerto Rico who yelled instructions in Spanish and carried a picture of Heifetz in his jacket pocket. Somehow it all added up to the beginning of a life-long love affair with classical music.

One of the few constants in Hyung Goo's checkered college career was his musical involvement: membership in the Harvard-Radcliffe Collegium Musicum and the University Choir, an assistant conductorship of the Harvard Glee Club, a brief stint as a music major, fleeting ambitions of a career as a conductor. Eventually, aspirations to a career in music gave way to a more realistic intention of becoming a physician. That plan was scuttled by HIV, and for a time, even music fell by the wayside.

As Hyung Goo moved back toward life in the wake of his HIV diagnosis, he moved back toward music. He played chamber music with friends from church: violin and piano sonatas, piano trios, string quartets. In the spring of 1989, he successfully auditioned for the Tanglewood Festival Chorus, the resident chorus of the Boston Symphony Orchestra. He had sung with the chorus once before, in the summer of 1977, as an extra singer for an immense performance at Tanglewood of the Berlioz *Requiem*. The concert had taken place on the day that Elvis died. Hyung Goo wrote in his memoir, "I can remember exactly where I was when I heard the news (whoopee)."

Hyung Goo sang with the chorus for two winter and summer seasons, until we married and he moved to North Carolina to be with me. Our courtship was filled with attendance
at his rehearsals and performances: a Mendelssohn oratorio
and the Verdi *Te Deum* in the spring of 1990, scenes from
Verdi and Tchaikovsky operas at Tanglewood that summer, the
Beethoven *Choral Fantasy* at Carnegie Hall in December, the
Brahms *Requiem* and symphonies by Beethoven and Mahler
at Tanglewood the next summer.

After the richness of Boston, Durham seemed a cultural
wasteland. Announcers at the only classical music station on
the FM dial mispronounced names of composers and performers, then played single movements of longer works. Subscrip-
tion series concerts at Duke seemed to be attended primarily
by people who had retired to Durham from elsewhere. There
were no students in attendance except the ushers; we were
always the youngest people there. Duke itself had no orchestra,
no chamber groups, apparently no string players at all. We felt
like we had left civilization itself behind.

Our twice-yearly trips to Boston took on the character of
musical pilgrimages. On the way, we would stop in New York.
One of Hyung Goo's college roommates had been a bass player
with an extensive collection of classical recordings. Frank went
on to become an economist with the Federal Reserve Bank in
New York. He developed a passion for opera, and bought an
apartment across the street from Lincoln Center so that he and
his wife could go to the opera every weekend. On our visits to
New York, we would attend a concert at Lincoln Center, after
which Frank and Hyung Goo would spend an evening engaged
in arcane conversation about which conductors and performers each of them preferred for what repertoire, and why.

From New York, we would go on to Boston. In the summer,
we would go to Tanglewood. In the winter, Hyung Goo would
try to arrange to sing in a performance or two of Christmas
Pops. Ordinarily, Christmas Pops is a kind of musical purga-
tory—you stand on stage singing the latest John Williams
sound-alike and listening to some of the best musicians in
the world playing "Waltzing in a Winter Wonderland," but it's

worth it because you get to sing good music the rest of the year. But for Hyung Goo, Christmas Pops came to seem one of his last connections to a world of tuxedos and concert halls, of real music and real musicians.

By the time Hyung Goo retired from his job, we had become more aware of what musical opportunities existed in Durham. There was a very fine choral conductor at Duke, and we both joined an undergraduate choral group that he conducted. Later we participated in an early-music ensemble that was led by an accomplished Russian-Israeli fortepianist and harpsichordist. But all our music-making in Durham was tinged with mourning for Boston, for the chorus, the symphony, the scores of musical friends and colleagues, the musical culture that had been to us, and to Hyung Goo especially, as natural and as all-encompassing as the air we breathed, and apart from which we felt ourselves perpetually at a loss.

As powerful a presence as music was in our life together, it was perhaps even more powerful as a metaphor for that life. Lyricist Jane Griner, in the words of a song by her husband, composer Daniel Gawthrop, writes,

> In my heart's sequestered chambers
> lie truths stripped of poet's gloss.
> Words alone are vain and vacant
> and my heart is mute.
>
> In response to aching silence
> memory summons half-heard voices,
> and my heart finds primal eloquence
> and wraps me in song.
>
> If you would comfort me, sing me a lullaby.
> If you would win my heart, sing me a love song.
> If you would mourn me and bring me to God
> sing me a requiem; sing me to heaven.

Hyung Goo's and my life together was such a three-fold song. Together each of us gave and received comfort, offered and received love, grieved for and was mourned by the other. Our life was a lullaby, a love song, a requiem; yet not three separate songs but one song, in a kind of musical vestige of the Trinity.

We had worried, when we were considering marrying one another, that Hyung Goo's eventual need for care in illness would make it difficult for us to develop a truly adult relationship with one another. I didn't want to be Hyung Goo's mother. I wanted to be his wife, and he wanted to be my husband, not my child. We found, as we moved through our marriage, that our relationship did develop a maternal dimension; but it was one in which the mothering ran in both directions, and which represented not a detraction from our intimacy as husband and wife, but a broadening and a deepening of that intimacy.

This maternal aspect of our relationship began to emerge in a particularly noticeable way in the spring of 1995, when Hyung Goo was in the hospital. The nurses had no time to care for their patients, so it fell to me to bathe him. As I washed him as a mother does her child, I was struck by the newness and the unfamiliarity of this kind of touch, so different from the physical interaction one has with a lover. Not long afterwards, I had a dream in which I was sitting in a rocking chair with Hyung Goo. He had his arms around me, and was rocking me to sleep. Even as I had bathed him, so he was comforting me, creating within his embrace a safe and quiet place in which I knew only that he was taking care of me.

We were both looking for a love affair when we began our courtship. We wanted affection and companionship and romance, and we got them; but we got something far deeper and more transformative as well. The spring before our marriage, I was at Duke and Hyung Goo was still in Boston. On Valentine's Day, Hyung Goo sent me flowers (which I had expected) and a box of chocolates (which I hadn't). As I opened the package the mailman had brought and discovered its contents, I felt I had been waiting for that box of chocolates my entire life. It was the beginning of a gift to me of my feminine self. I had always been quick to display qualities characterized as masculine: analytical and mathematical ability, a rationality seemingly detached from feeling. Femininity had seemed like something imposed from without, something that never seemed to fit, like a garment that droops or constrains. But as Hyung Goo drew me to himself, I discovered a femininity that seemed a very spring of being and of self, something that welled up from deep within and issued in abundance and life, a fecundity not only surprising but paradoxical, given the much-sorrowed-over childlessness of our marriage.

And it was in the context of our marriage that Hyung Goo took possession of his own masculinity. The dislocations and deprivations of Hyung Goo's early life, acting on his naturally sensitive temperament, had issued in a terribly fragile and damaged sense of self. He longed desperately for relationship, and yet could not bring himself to believe that he was what any woman would want. When Hyung Goo first told me the story of his sexual misadventures, either I asked, or he was trying to explain, why he did these things. "At least I felt that these people wanted to be with me," he said. "At least I felt that they found me attractive." Like Max in *Where the Wild Things Are*, Hyung Goo wanted most just to be where someone loved him best of all. In our marriage he found that place. I couldn't have loved him more if there had been ten of me. And the more I loved him, and the more I relaxed into his love for me, the more worthwhile and competent he felt; until in the last years of his life he had settled into a confident, gentle, joyful sense of himself as a man and as a husband.

From the day I learned of Hyung Goo's HIV infection, I resented the way that sorrow and grief overshadowed our relationship. "Illness and death are for old people," I thought with the callousness so characteristic of the young and healthy. "I shouldn't have to deal with anything like this for at least fifty years." But we did have to deal with it; and mourning became as integral a part of our life together as the love we wanted and the comfort we found along the way. We mourned for the children we knew we would never have. We mourned for the many years together that we knew we could not hope for. I grieved in the knowledge that I would lose Hyung Goo and the life we had made together. Hyung Goo grieved the fact that he would miss sharing in so much of my life, and would die not knowing so much of my story. And both of us grieved his anticipated death itself, the fact that he would have to relinquish life and all the good things of life so long before it seemed fitting that he should do so.

We began to see only gradually and toward the end of Hyung Goo's life the ways in which the present and anticipated grief of our marriage had contributed to the richness of our life together. The sorrows of our life had not simply detracted from our happiness, but had shaped and even contributed to that happiness. In the spring of 1995, it was becoming clear that Hyung Goo was not going to live much longer—maybe a year, probably less. In the midst of his worsening illness, he and I were coping together in much more cooperative and mutually supportive ways than in former days. "It really is remarkable how far you two have come in just four years," Martha commented to me.

She was right; but I wanted more. Where might we have been in ten years, if we had them?

"It is fruitless to ask that question," Martha said. "If you had ever thought you had that kind of time, you wouldn't be where you are now."

It was impossible to see AIDS itself as a good. But it was equally impossible to see that the particular good that Hyung Goo and I had experienced together in the midst of AIDS could have been obtained in any other way. The requiem that we sang for one another and with one another was not something external to our marriage, like a piece of black crape draped over the frame of an otherwise sunny and cheerful picture. Our individual and shared sorrows were part of the picture itself, shadows without which the picture and its characteristic beauty would have been, if not gone, then at least altered beyond recognition.

The lullabys and love songs with which we comforted and courted one another were mostly metaphorical, but the requiems were literal as well as figurative. The last of them was in August of 1995, only six weeks (as it turned out) before Hyung

Goo died. The Tanglewood Festival Chorus was celebrating its twenty-fifth season with two major works for chorus and orchestra: the Berlioz *Requiem*, one of the great settings of the classic Latin text of the Requiem Mass, and the Mahler *Symphony No. 2*, nicknamed "The Resurrection" for its text emphasizing the Christian hope of the resurrection of the dead. We knew of these concerts well in advance, and longed to go to them (and to the party with all our chorus friends that would accompany them), but traveling to Tanglewood for the weekend from North Carolina would require plane tickets and a rental car and a hotel stay. It would be impossibly expensive.

Then one of Hyung Goo's aunts gave us a check for $1,000. I was instantly on the phone making plane reservations. Added incentive for making the trip despite Hyung Goo's precarious state of health was the fact that Hyung Goo's brother and his wife were expecting their third child in July. We could go a few days early and meet the baby. Who knew when our next opportunity might be? While we were at it, we called the cemetery and arranged to have our gravestone laid. We didn't think Hyung Goo would be dying right away, but we wanted the stone on the grave before he was buried. If we did it now, it would be done, and we could go and see it when we were in Boston.

Hyung Goo's niece, Teresa, was born on July 8. Three weeks later we flew to Boston. We went first to the cemetery, where we found the gravestone had been laid that morning. "I know that my Redeemer liveth," it said across the top, echoing both the aria from *Messiah* and the book of Job. Below were Hyung Goo's name and date of birth, with a space to the right of the inscription for his date of death, and space below that for my name and dates of birth and death. What are you supposed to do when you visit your own grave? Hyung Goo sat on the ground by the stone, and I took a picture.

We went on to Hyung Goo's brother's home. Hyung Goo sat in an armchair, cradling the baby, drifting in and out of sleep. We had brought books as gifts for Hyung Goo's three- and five-year-old nephews. By the time we left, I had read *Bread and Jam for Frances* more times than I cared to remember. We didn't talk much with Hyung Goo's brother and his wife, but it didn't seem to matter. We were there, and that was enough for all of us.

A day or two later we went to Tanglewood. The performance of the Berlioz was on Saturday evening. The words and music were accompanied by the rumbling of thunder and the steady rhythm of rain. *"Requiem aeternam dona defunctis, Domine, et lux perpetua luceat eis."* "Grant the dead eternal rest, O Lord, and may perpetual light shine upon them." After the performance we picked our way over muddy ground to the tent where the anniversary party was underway. We shouted over the noise with our friends; there were speeches and toasts in honor of the chorus and the chorus master; everyone sang a silly song written in honor of the occasion.

The Mahler was on Sunday afternoon. Overnight, rain had given way to sunshine. *"Auferstehn, ja auferstehn wirst du, mein Staub, nach kurzer Ruh!"* "Rise again, yet rise again you will, my dust, after brief repose," announced the chorus. *"O glaube, du warst nicht umsonst geboren! Hast nicht umsonst gelebt, gelitten!"* "Believe that you were not born in vain, that you have not vainly lived and suffered," responded the soprano soloist. We lingered after the concert, visiting with a friend who had traveled to attend the concert with us. Finally, it was time to leave. We drove back to Boston. Two days later, having in less than a week made the rounds from death to birth to resurrection and eternal life, we flew home to North Carolina.

A week or two later, the telephone rang. It was Frank. He was traveling somewhere and had time on his hands. He was calling from a pay phone, just to talk. He had recently heard the most marvelous performance of the Berlioz *Requiem* on a live radio broadcast from Tanglewood. Had Hyung Goo perhaps heard the same broadcast?

"I was there!" Hyung Goo said.

# JANUARY 6, 1994:
# CMV DIAGNOSIS

Most of the opportunistic infections that are associated with AIDS are caused not by exotic or virulent germs that would make anyone sick, but by microorganisms that virtually everyone is exposed to but that cause illness only in persons with compromised immune systems. Cytomegalovirus is one such microorganism. In people with AIDS, it tends to take up residence in the retina, where it kills cells and thus impairs vision in a condition called CMV retinitis. The progression of CMV retinitis can be slowed but not stopped by medication. As Martha told me some time after Hyung Goo's death, "What we say is, 'You have to take this drug for the rest of your life.' What we don't say is, 'And if you live long enough, you will go blind.'"

In January of 1994, Hyung Goo went to the clinic for a regularly scheduled checkup. John looked into Hyung Goo's right eye and saw what looked to him like evidence of CMV retinitis. Hyung Goo was seen that afternoon on an emergency basis at the Duke retina clinic, where a chief resident confirmed the diagnosis. The next day Hyung Goo began treatment with intravenous Ganciclovir.

There had been a time not too far in the past when the law did not permit IV medication to be administered by anyone but a trained nurse. Anyone who needed daily intravenous medication had three choices: be admitted to the hospital, hire a nurse to administer the medication at home, or enter a nursing home. To people with AIDS or cancer or any one of a number of other illnesses who were not sick enough to be in the hospital, did not have the means to hire a private nurse, and were perfectly capable of living in their own homes, these all looked like bad choices. Under pressure from patient advocacy groups, regulations began to change, and home health agencies began supporting what was called "home infusion therapy."

Home infusion therapy would be impractical if a patient were required to find a vein with a needle every time he or she administered an IV. A prerequisite for home infusion therapy is thus the placing of an IV catheter. This is a tube that enters a blood vessel in the arm or chest and has a valve and clamp arrangement on the end that remains outside the body. Medication is administered by attaching one end of an IV tube to the bag containing the medicine, and the other end to the valved end of the catheter.

Hyung Goo's CMV diagnosis came on a Thursday. On Friday, we went in to the clinic, where a temporary IV line was placed in Hyung Goo's hand, and his first dose of Ganciclovir administered through it. At the same time, Martha and Trish sat down with us to discuss the options for a permanent IV catheter. Hyung Goo already felt anxious and upset about his CMV diagnosis, and was not happy at being pressed for an immediate decision about the catheter. But Martha and Trish needed an answer so they could make arrangements to have the catheter inserted on Monday. With ill grace, Hyung Goo opted for a Hickman central line, and the appointment with surgical radiology was made.

The Hickman line was inserted under local anesthetic. Hyung Goo watched on the x-ray screen as the radiologist inserted the tubing through an incision on the left side of his chest and snaked it around until the end of it rested in the superior vena cava, on the right side of his heart. After the procedure, he was wheeled on a stretcher into the recovery room, where I was allowed to see him. Sure that I would take as academic an interest in his catheter as he did, Hyung Goo raised himself on one elbow, and with his other hand pulled back the dressing so I could see the insertion site. I immediately turned gray and had to sit down on the floor of the recovery

97

room, where nurses rushed over to me, proffering cups of apple juice.

For all his unhappiness at being pressed for a decision about the catheter, Hyung Goo came to love his Hickman line. He received all his IV medication through it, not only Ganciclovir but also the chemotherapy drugs used to treat his Kaposi's sarcoma, most of which were so caustic that they caused pain and swelling in his arm when given via a traditional IV. Blood transfusions and other IV fluids could be given through the Hickman line; blood draws could be taken through it. It was the end of being stuck with needles every time he turned around.

Hyung Goo managed the catheter with meticulous attention to sterile technique. When he changed his dressing, he would put on a surgical mask and stand in front of the bathroom mirror as he scrubbed the area around the insertion site with cleansing and antiseptic swabs and applied the new dressing. When he administered his medication, he would sit at the dining-room table with the IV bag hanging from the curtain rod behind him and his supplies laid out on the table before him: coils of IV tubing, alcohol swabs, syringes of Heparin (a blood thinner used to keep the catheter from clotting off). Once everything was all hooked up, he would move into the living room so he could watch TV while the medicine ran in. There was no curtain rod in convenient proximity to the television, but on the wall was a photograph of my grandmother, in an old-fashioned frame that stuck out from the wall. I glued the picture to the wall so it wouldn't tilt, and Hyung Goo hung the IV on the picture frame.

Hyung Goo took two doses a day of Ganciclovir for two weeks, and then scaled back to one dose a day, five days a week. In those first two weeks, it seemed as if every time we wanted to go anywhere or do anything, we couldn't, because Hyung Goo had to do his medicine. We were relieved when he cut back to the maintenance dose, and doubly relieved when an examination at the retina clinic indicated that the spread of the CMV seemed to have been stopped. A couple of months later, the ophthalmologist saw new evidence of CMV activity in Hyung Goo's right eye. He went back on a twice-a-day induction dose

98

for another two weeks, and then resumed maintenance therapy at the higher level of one dose a day, seven days a week.

This pattern continued for the remainder of Hyung Goo's life. A given dose of Ganciclovir would keep the CMV in check for a period of time. Then the infection would reactivate and he would lose more vision. At one point he tried another medication, Foscarnet, but its side effects were so severe they almost killed him. The only thing to do was to take more and more Ganciclovir—a longer induction dose, a higher maintenance dose. One of those periods of induction came in the summer of 1995. Hooking up the IV twice a day didn't seem nearly as obtrusive as it had a year and a half earlier, when he first received his CMV diagnosis. The reason, I realized, was that in January of 1994, we were busy with classes and church activities and a host of other things that the Ganciclovir routine interrupted. By the summer of 1995, we weren't doing anything but managing Hyung Goo's health. There wasn't anything for the Ganciclovir to interrupt.

Hyung Goo's CMV diagnosis brought with it a host of small adjustments, one major explosion, and a nagging existential issue. The small adjustments included learning how to administer the medication and change the dressing, making room in our daily routine for the time it all took, rearranging the refrigerator to make a place to keep the several weeks' supply of Ganciclovir that the home health agency would deliver at one time, and becoming accustomed to the fact of the catheter itself. There was no pain or any other sensation involved in its presence, but having sixteen inches of rubber tubing perpetually protruding from Hyung Goo's chest took some getting used to.

The explosion had to do with the pricing of the medication. The home health agency that delivered Hyung Goo's Ganciclovir and all his associated IV supplies billed our insurance company directly and was reimbursed directly in turn. It was two or three months before we received claim forms from the insurance company documenting what the home health agency had billed and been reimbursed for. They were charging over $500 a dose, more than $20,000 on the first claim form alone.

Hyung Goo was shocked. He had been warned that Ganciclovir was expensive, but he couldn't believe it was that expensive. He called the other home infusion company in the area, and got a quote for $178 a dose. Now he wasn't just shocked; he was outraged. He got the manager of our home health company on the telephone, and gave him an earful about what he saw as price gouging. Cowed by Hyung Goo's ire, the manager offered to reduce the charges retroactively to $225 a dose.

"That's not good enough," Hyung Goo said.

In the end, our home health agency matched the other company's price of $178 a dose. Hyung Goo wrote a letter to our insurance company, instructing them to make no further payments to the home health agency until the billing issues were resolved, and chastising them for having paid without question such inflated claims in the first place. "Who is minding the store?" Hyung Goo asked testily.

Controlling his medication costs was an intensely practical matter—Hyung Goo's insurance policy had a $1,000,000 lifetime cap, and he didn't want to take any chances that he would exceed his lifetime maximum. But the CMV diagnosis had existential as well as practical consequences. CMV retinitis is "statistically correlated with end-stage HIV disease." In plain language, this means that a person with CMV retinitis is typically in the last year of his or her life. Was this true of Hyung Goo? Were we that near the end? It didn't seem like Hyung Goo was at death's door. Most days he was just fine. On the other hand, we realized, it wouldn't take much for him to be not fine at all. Should we be ready for him to die? What would being ready look like?

We started to plan his funeral.

# MARCH 14, 1994:
# PCP DIAGNOSIS

One of the most characteristic of AIDS-related conditions is Pneumocystis carinii pneumonia, or PCP. Pneumocystis carinii, the microorganism that causes this particular kind of pneumonia, is another of the many bugs to which most people are exposed, but which sicken only people with compromised immune systems. PCP comes on slowly and responds slowly to treatment. As a result, a person who has PCP has often been sick for some time before a diagnosis is made, and may continue to get worse for awhile even after treatment is begun. If a person is already gravely ill before PCP is diagnosed, there may be no room to get worse before getting better—hence the status of PCP as a leading cause of death among people with AIDS.

A month or so after Hyung Goo had begun treatment for CMV, he started running fevers. They were just little fevers at first. We hardly noticed when they began. Hyung Goo was receiving periodic chemotherapy for his KS at the time. Were the fevers a reaction to the chemo? Or were they associated with his CMV, or perhaps with his HIV infection itself? Or were they symptomatic of something worse, like PCP? The more fevers Hyung Goo had, and the higher they got, the more I suspected he had PCP. Nonsense, Hyung Goo said. If he had PCP, he would be really sick, which he wasn't. He had everything under control. I should stop worrying.

101

Finally, even Hyung Goo couldn't deny that something really was wrong. He went in to the clinic on a Friday, where a chest x-ray showed "diffuse infiltration," meaning that his lungs had little spots all over them. The doctor who saw Hyung Goo explained that merely on the basis of the x-ray, she couldn't say whether the spots were caused by pneumonia or by something else, like KS or tuberculosis, but given the high fevers he had been running, it was probably pneumonia. Hyung Goo's blood oxygen levels were close to normal, so the doctor didn't insist that he be admitted to the hospital. She gave us strict instructions to go straight to the emergency room if Hyung Goo felt "poorly" over the weekend, and scheduled a procedure for Monday to confirm the diagnosis so that treatment could be begun.

We went home, where Hyung Goo lay on the couch, breathing shallowly and coughing and burning with fever, and insisting that he did not feel poorly and did not need to go to the hospital. On Sunday, he woke up with chills. As his fever mounted to 102°, 103°, 104°, 105°, I said in panicked tones, "We need to go to the emergency room."

"Absolutely not," said Hyung Goo through chattering teeth. "I am just fine. I have everything under control."

The fever came down, and we ended up going to church, with me absolutely furious with Hyung Goo for frightening me and for being so pigheaded. I marched into church by myself and sat down next to a friend with whom I had spoken on the telephone earlier that morning while Hyung Goo was having his fever and refusing to go to the emergency room. Assuming I was there alone, she turned to me and said, "Are you pissed?" Toward the end of the service, she caught sight of Hyung Goo sitting on the other side of the aisle, by himself. She looked at me and said, "You *are* pissed!"

On Monday we went to the hospital for Hyung Goo's scheduled bronchoscopy. Hyung Goo lay on a table while the pulmonologist threaded a tube through his nose and down into his lungs to retrieve a sputum sample that could be tested for the presence of *Pneumocystis carinii*. As the procedure ended,

Hyung Goo started to chill. As he lay there shaking, the pulmonologist said, "What's happening?"

"I'm having a chill," Hyung Goo replied.

"Oh," said the pulmonologist, looking blank and a little uncomfortable, like he had never been around a sick person before and didn't much like it.

Hyung Goo's fever mounted quickly. It was clear that no one in pulmonology knew what to do. "Get me an orderly and a wheelchair, now!" I said. The orderly and I lifted Hyung Goo off the table and into the wheelchair, and wheeled him down the hall to the ID clinic. They had seen sick people before, and they did know what to do. They put him in one of the reclining chairs in the clinic treatment room, dosed him up with Tylenol and Ibuprofen, and waited for the fever to come down. It reached 107° before it broke. The doctor and nurse who were caring for Hyung Goo moved softly in and out of the room, checking Hyung Goo's temperature, administering more drugs every couple of hours, hovering gently over both of us. By the end of the afternoon, the fever had abated. We staggered home, thankful only to have escaped being admitted. The next day John called with the results of the bronchoscopy. It was PCP.

PCP brought three new things into our lives: a new roster of medications, fever as a constant companion, and the palpable specter of death. Standard treatment for PCP was a sulfa drug to which Hyung Goo was allergic. An alternative was intravenous Pentamidine. Hyung Goo had been breathing in an aerosolized form of Pentamidine once a month for a year and a half or so in an effort to prevent PCP altogether. Aerosolized Pentamidine was not unpleasant, but IV Pentamidine had a lot of nasty side effects, including nausea and vomiting. A new drug, Mepron, had many fewer side effects and had shown promising results in clinical trials. John suggested that Hyung Goo try Mepron first and see how it worked.

Not well enough, was the final answer. Hyung Goo took Mepron for two weeks, and then resumed preventive treatment every two weeks with aerosolized Pentamidine. After a few weeks, he started running fevers again. The PCP was back. He went back on Mepron for a month; again, symptoms abated while he was on Mepron but returned once he stopped taking it. He and John gave Mepron one more try, for six weeks this time. The same thing happened. By this time it was the middle of the summer, and we were in Boston. The primary care physician whom Hyung Goo was seeing there wouldn't take Hyung Goo's word for it that his PCP was recurring, and ordered various tests, all of which came back with inconclusive results. "Let's wait and see if you get sicker," the doctor said.

That wasn't something we felt like waiting for. With visions of Hyung Goo becoming so sick he couldn't travel, we threw our things into the car and drove back to North Carolina a week or two earlier than we had planned. Sure enough, it was PCP. In a last-ditch attempt to keep Hyung Goo off IV Pentamidine, John tried Clindamycin. Hyung Goo had an allergic reaction to it, and ended up on IV Pentamidine after all. This was not a drug that could be administered at home, so for two weeks Hyung Goo went in to the clinic every day and received his medication there. By the end of the two weeks, he was so nauseated he could hardly eat. When he did eat, he threw up. We started watching TV while we ate, just to keep Hyung Goo's mind off his nausea.

IV Pentamidine proved a better drug for PCP than Mepron had been, but even it wasn't good enough. Hyung Goo had PCP on and off again for the rest of his life. Sometimes it was months rather than weeks after a course of medication before symptoms recurred, but they did recur, time and time again.

The most immediately obvious symptom of PCP was fever. We learned a few things from the 107° fever that consumed Hyung Goo in the wake of his bronchoscopy. Hyung Goo's preferred coping mechanism to that point had been to deny ever feeling ill, and to insist that he was in control of any apparent symptoms. My preferred coping mechanism had been always to imagine the worst, and to try to strongarm Hyung Goo into doing whatever I thought best. The bronchoscopy episode was the end of all that. Hyung Goo realized (he told Martha, penitently, a week or so later) that sometimes I knew better than he did just how sick he was. For my part, I realized that I had

104

had no idea what to do. If we were going to learn to deal with fever, we were going to have to do so together.

Hyung Goo would often start to chill early in the morning. He would take some Tylenol and lie in bed under piles of covers to stay warm. As soon as he stopped chilling, I would get a basin of water and start sponging him. The fever wouldn't have peaked yet, and the sponging helped keep the fever from getting as high as it might have otherwise, and helped it come down more quickly once it broke. It was also a positive, intimate way to experience together something that otherwise had nothing to recommend it. We would take his temperature every twenty minutes or so as we waited for the fever to come down. It could take hours. Every two hours he would take another dose of medication, alternating Ibuprofen with Tylenol. Once his temperature reached 101° or so, I would stop sponging. Hyung Goo might sleep for awhile, and then he would get up and go about his business, often feeling better enough that it seemed hard to believe that he had been so sick earlier in the day.

The fever Hyung Goo had on June 8, 1994, was typical. It was notable only because the day was our third wedding anniversary. The day began at 5:30 with chills and a fever of 104.9°. This was the morning we figured out that it was imperative that Hyung Goo sit up and take his medicine as soon as he started to chill. If he waited, he would be too weak to do so until after the chill was over, and as a consequence the fever would be higher and take longer to come down. I spent an hour and a half sponging him, and then we both got a couple more hours of sleep. By the afternoon, Hyung Goo felt tired but otherwise fine. He dropped me off for my appointment with Dan and went to run errands. In the evening, we went to dinner at a fancy Italian restaurant in a neighboring town, and celebrated our anniversary.

That day was typical in a broader sense as well. The juxtaposition of the terrifying, the mundane, and the joyful came to characterize nearly the whole of our life, post-PCP. Hyung Goo's diagnosis with CMV had made us wonder whether death might be just around the corner. With his diagnosis with PCP, we knew it was. For the first time, Hyung Goo was sick with something that could kill him. The fevers, the nausea, the exhaustion and shortness of breath and collapsed lungs (which came later) were all reminders that we were no longer waiting to see what awful thing might happen. It had started to happen already.

But alongside the awfulness, all the everyday details of life were still there to be lived: errands to run, appointments to keep, meals to be cooked and eaten. And in the midst of it all, the dramatic and the pedestrian alike, our marriage bloomed, like a little flower in the midst of a desert.

# OUT OF CONTACT

One morning, midway through the summer of 1994, I awoke, gasping for breath, from a dream in which I had begun as the sole passenger in a small boat in the middle of the ocean. The boat—a mere rowboat, really—had lost radio contact with the mainland. In an effort to reestablish contact, I jumped out of the boat carrying the radio transmitter, intending to swim with it to shore. Instead, I found myself dragged down by the weight of the transmitter deep into the ocean, far enough down that I could feel the weight and pressure of the water squeezing the life and breath out of me, far enough down that I knew I could never get up to the surface again.

I had had lots of drowning-in-the-ocean dreams before. Always before, I had stayed more or less on the surface. I didn't like this latest twist at all. After a few minutes of lying in bed shaking, I called Dan.

"So what do you think this is all about?" Dan asked.

"I think it means I'm out of town and my therapist is in North Carolina!" I said.

"Well, yes," said Dan.

# SOME PEOPLE

Hyung Goo and I spent the summer of 1994 in Boston. We thought of it as a respite from our exile in Durham: an opportunity to reconnect with the culture and geography of Boston as well as with the friends and family whom it seemed there was never enough time to see on our more usual brief trips. We seem also to have imagined that the summer would somehow be a respite from illness. If we can just get back to Boston, we thought, things will be the way they used to be, the way they were before Hyung Goo got sick.

Of course they weren't. For the first two weeks we were in Boston, we did nothing but eat, sleep, and drag around from doctor to doctor, making the first round of appointments with all the new providers whom Hyung Goo had arranged to see while we were there: primary-care physician, ophthalmologist, oncologists. What had happened to our fantasy of a leisurely vacation? There we were, surrounded by people we wanted to see and things we wanted to do, and we were spending all our time at hospitals talking to crowds of doctors or at home monitoring fevers or administering IV medication.

Eventually we did muster the energy to get on the telephone and call people, and our summer entered phase two: dinner out every night of the week with a different person or couple, mostly accompanied by long intense conversations of the kind people have with you when you haven't seen them in a long time and they (or you) are afraid they may never see you again. "In case you've never tried to socialize on this scale," I wrote to a friend, "let me tell you: it is a bad idea. I am wired to deal with one or two intense conversations a week, not one or two a day. I think that when the summer is over, I would like to retreat somewhere, like the Egyptian desert, and sit under a bush for a month or two without talking to anybody."

We also spent time with family. We were living upstairs from Hyung Goo's parents, and saw them every day. Every time I talked with Hyung Goo's mother, she wanted to know how he was doing. I could hear the fear in her voice and see it in her face—the fear of a mother about to lose her son. Even happy occasions were upsetting. Hyung Goo's nephew Andrew celebrated his fourth birthday in mid-July. His birthday cake was shaped like an elephant, with M&Ms for toenails, which his two-year-old brother, Nathan, picked off and ate one by one before the candles got lit and blown out. Both nephews were adorable. They were also inescapable reminders that Hyung Goo's brothers had children and we didn't.

I spent a good portion of the summer coming apart at the seams. One morning soon after our arrival, I was hanging out the laundry on my in-laws' highly unsatisfactory clothesline with their highly unsatisfactory clothespins, and I was nearly in tears. Then I went upstairs and cooked Hyung Goo's breakfast and broke one of his eggs getting it out of the pan, and I really did burst into tears. I sat at the kitchen table and sobbed, with Hyung Goo looking at me over his egg. In the afternoon I was in tears again because Hyung Goo wanted to move a bookcase from one room to another, and again because of some electrical wiring that was not as it should have been. Successive days and weeks were much the same.

Dan had seen some of this coming, and had suggested I continue therapy with him over the telephone for the course of the summer. I thought therapy by telephone sounded completely ridiculous, but it didn't take me long to realize I wasn't going to make it through the summer without it. When Dan himself went on vacation, he sent me a letter with his itinerary and telephone numbers where he could be reached on any given day. "I've never seen a therapist make himself this available to a client," Hyung Goo said, looking over Dan's letter. The summer began to resemble a giant outtake from *What About*

109

*Bob?* as my overwrought phone calls followed Dan from North Carolina to Indiana and back.

"I feel such an acute sense of loss over everything," I wrote to Dan, between phone calls. "Being in Boston just makes it worse, because we're confronted with all these things we want to do, and if we don't do them now, we'll never do them—and most of them we can't do, because there are too many, and, anyway, we're too tired. So I look around at everything and everyone, and I feel overwhelmed and suffocated and panicky, and all I want to do is cry. Life is too short; time is too short; what little we have left is slipping away from us, and I can almost feel it going. It is like having my insides slowly disappear; there is less and less inside, and I am doubling over from the emptiness, less and less cognizant of anything but loss."

For all that, it was a good summer. Hyung Goo was deeply happy at being back in Boston. He played in a summer chamber orchestra in Cambridge; we watched the Harborfest fireworks from the Charlestown Navy Yard; we walked around Harvard Square in the evenings, watching the chess players and the street entertainers. At the same time, we both began to realize that as much as we loved Boston, it really was not home anymore. When we returned to Durham at the end of the summer, it was with a sense of relief at being back where our life was.

The summer also gave us an opportunity to take advantage of the medical resources that Boston had to offer. Hyung Goo was particularly concerned to investigate treatment options for his Kaposi's sarcoma. He had undergone some chemotherapy for the KS over the previous year and had not tolerated the drugs well at all. The oncologist seemed not to have any other ideas about what to do, and there wasn't anyone else to consult with in Durham. In Boston, there were whole teams of physicians who specialized in the treatment of KS. Hyung Goo arranged to be seen by one such team, at Beth Israel Hospital, in the hope that they would have knowledge of other possible treatment regimens.

The oncologists at Beth Israel treated Hyung Goo as a colleague. They gave him hours of their time, talking with him not only about treatment options for his KS but about his entire medical situation, thinking with him about pain control, medication for nausea and fever, his falling blood counts, his sulfa allergies. The senior oncologist took a detailed enough history that he learned about Hyung Goo's research at Mass. General. When we came for our next appointment, he had looked up and read a paper that Hyung Goo had coauthored. He and Hyung Goo sat and talked about it as Hyung Goo received his dose of chemotherapy.

The oncology clinic itself was an instructive contrast to Duke's medical oncology clinic. At Duke, medical oncology patients were routinely kept waiting for hours beyond their scheduled appointment times, and were seen by different nurses and aides at every visit, with the result that they experienced no continuity of care. At Beth Israel, each patient was assigned to a nurse, scheduled for appointments only when that nurse was working, and seen within twenty minutes of the scheduled time as a matter of policy. The staff of the Duke clinic seemed to suppose that the chaos within which they operated was somehow inevitable. Beth Israel showed that it was possible to run such a clinic well.

On the other hand, things just took so much longer in Boston. Hyung Goo had become severely anemic and thus transfusion-dependent late in the spring, requiring a couple of units of packed red blood cells every two or three weeks. One day we went to Beth Israel for a blood transfusion. We were there from 2:30 in the afternoon until 8:30 that evening. The nurses wouldn't run in a unit of red cells in less than two hours. Quite understandably, they didn't want anyone dying of heart failure or an allergic reaction in the middle of a transfusion. But at Duke, where Hyung Goo knew the nurses, he could sweet-talk them into running in two units of red cells in just over an hour. We could have flown to North Carolina, gotten the blood transfusion, and flown back to Boston in less time than it took to get the blood at Beth Israel.

And it wasn't just blood transfusions that were less convenient. The various doctors whom Hyung Goo was seeing were in different places all over greater Boston. All the locations

111

were at least a half an hour from where we were living, and parking was nonexistent, impossibly expensive, or both. In Durham, everything was in the same place, five minutes from our home, with a parking garage next door. As helpful as it had been to consult with the doctors at Beth Israel about his KS, Hyung Goo realized over the course of the summer how well situated we were in Durham. Duke might not have everything to offer that the entire city of Boston did, but the medicine being practiced at the ID clinic was personal, attentive, and utterly professional, and it was just across the street.

Ultimately, the summer was about people. Charlotte Zolotow writes,

> Some people laugh and laugh
> and yet you want to cry.
> Some people touch your hand
> and music fills the sky.

Somehow we ended up with way more than our share of the second sort of people. Over the course of the summer, we had meals or conversations with at least seventy friends, and there were still some whom we didn't get to see. I groused to Dan all summer long about how overloaded my circuits were, not because I wished we had fewer friends, but because I wished there were more time to spend with them. I realized in the course of every conversation that I didn't know this person nearly well enough, and wished I could talk with him or her at this length and depth every week for a year, only of course I couldn't. There was no time; life was too short, and we were too far away.

It was wrenching to realize how much we would never know about all of these people who loved us. It was wrenching, too, to begin to see our friends' own sorrows and brokenness and limitations more clearly. All my life I had dealt with my own pains and complexities by rejecting and ignoring them. As I began, through both therapy and marriage, to take my own shadow side more seriously, lo and behold, I discovered I had been rejecting and ignoring everyone else's pains and complexities as well. Now, as Hyung Goo and I entered into deep and intimate conversation with one friend after another, those sorrows stepped one by one into view: that of the woman who had realized that she and her husband would never have the baby they longed for; of the man whose large Catholic family had been shaken to its foundations by the death of one of his brothers from AIDS; of the pastor who, despite his enormous capacity for kindness, had managed to alienate everyone he worked with; of the older couple whose daughters had married unwisely.

And yet, the overwhelming sense we had as we talked with our friends about their lives and about ours was not one of sorrow but of fullness. We had dinner one evening at the home of a semiretired dentist and his wife, both of whom I had known years before from church. Howard and Bobbie were great talkers, and we heard all the news about everyone we knew in common, plus a good many people we didn't know at all. After dinner, they told us about Howard's secretary's son, who had recently died of AIDS. They asked us about Hyung Goo's health, and about our marriage and future plans, insofar as we had any. As we talked and listened, I realized that the significance of the conversation lay less in what was said than in how we felt in the course of it and afterwards. We felt loved, and soothed, and thankful. As we left the house and got into our car, the first words out of Hyung Goo's mouth were, "I hope they live to be a hundred."

In the middle of the summer, we spent a week in New York, where Hyung Goo had an assortment of friends from college: a violinist, a physician, an economist, a filmmaker, a businesswoman. We met them for dinner and conversation at Korean restaurants all over Manhattan. The exception was the filmmaker, a Turk, who took us to a Turkish restaurant, where we ate fried liver cubes and marinated eggplant and almond pudding until we couldn't eat any more. I had friends in New York as well: a couple whose children I had babysat one summer fifteen years earlier. We had kept in touch only sporadically, but when they learned that Hyung Goo had AIDS, they opened their home and their lives to us, entertaining us for dinner that summer as they did every time we were in New York. We talked late into the evening about Jon's work as an attorney and a union actor, about Rosemary's work as a therapist and psychoanalyst, about our own interests and activities.

As the summer drew to a close, we made our way home along a route that included yet more friends. One of Hyung Goo's college roommates, a gentle Southerner, was a plasma physicist on the faculty at Princeton. His wife was an artist. She had recently moved from doing representational art to more abstract pieces, with the result, she said, that now neither of them understood the other's work. Both Greg and Kate understood well the arts of hospitality and friendship. They entertained us regularly on our journeys to and from Boston, and stayed with us on their journeys to and from Greg's family home in Georgia. This visit, like those that preceded and followed it, was filled with good food and conversation, as our differing interests and personalities wove together into a complex and multilayered four-way relationship. We did not know it at the time, but that friendship would be called upon to bear a heavy burden in the final weeks of Hyung Goo's life and in the first weeks of my widowhood.

# THE RHETORIC OF AIDS

There is something in AIDS to offend everyone. Social conservatives are appalled by the sexual licentiousness that facilitates the spread of AIDS. Social liberals are dismayed that something as good as sex could possibly have fatal consequences. And everyone in the modern West is offended by the idea that there could be such a thing as an infectious disease for which there is no ready cure. Our grandparents' generation died young, of pneumonia, influenza, tuberculosis. We think that if we have to die at all, it should be at a grand old age, and then only of some chronic ailment like cancer or heart disease. AIDS is thus not just an illness; it is a gauntlet thrown down before us, a challenge to all our comfortable assumptions about the way the world ought to be.

Perhaps this is why people tend to take AIDS so personally. We practically define ourselves in relation to it. Does AIDS happen to "us," or does it happen to "them"? For gay white men, AIDS has from early on been something that happens to "us." AIDS was first identified in young gay men in centers of gay culture like San Francisco and New York. As gay men began to recognize how many of their number were infected, ill, or dying, they made AIDS a rallying point, calling for better medical care and better access to care, for less-risky patterns of behavior, for a readiness to care for the sick and to mourn the dead. And, over against the condemnation and rejection that many of them had experienced from family, society, and the church, they sought for ways to affirm and understand the

115

value of their individual and corporate lives in the face of this terrible and overwhelming epidemic.

For a good many Christians, on the other hand, AIDS is something that happens to "them." Many conservative Christians have long been inclined to suppose that the worst sins are sexual, and the worst sexual sins are homosexual. Perhaps it is thus not surprising that many Christians seized on the early correlation of AIDS and homosexuality as sufficient reason to understand AIDS as a uniquely terrible fate that befalls uniquely wicked people. AIDS doesn't happen to nice people, decent people, Christian people. It happens to bad people, who deserve it. The so-called "innocent" victims of AIDS—hemophiliacs, infant children—are pathetic exceptions to the general rule: to have AIDS is to be guilty of something really bad. Thus, as the gay community responded to AIDS as an enemy requiring engagement, and as a call to affirm the value of their lives in the face of those (especially Christians) who would reject and condemn, large segments of the Christian community responded to AIDS as God's judgment on other people (especially homosexuals), as something to be feared and avoided but not encountered personally.

Hyung Goo and I felt ourselves caught in the crossfire between these opposing rhetorical camps. Neither the external (Christian) nor the internal (gay) rhetoric of AIDS paused long to consider the existence of happily married, conventionally Christian people living with AIDS. For the Christians, people with AIDS were the enemy, not members of the family. For the gay community, the institutions of marriage and the church were oppressive, irrelevant, or both. And yet, we were members both of the AIDS community and of the family of the church. We moved in both of these worlds, belonging to them by virtue of our obvious affiliations, and yet strangers by virtue of our other allegiances. Our dual citizenship made us aliens wherever we went, and caused us to listen simultaneously as insiders and as outsiders to the rhetoric of both worlds.

A dominant theme in too much Christian rhetoric concerning AIDS is that AIDS is primarily a moral problem, and a life of virtue will make the problem go away. In the summer of 1994, the evangelical Christian group Focus on the Family published a full-page newspaper ad headlined, "In Defense of a Little Virginity," the burden of which was that all the condoms in the world wouldn't keep you from coming down with AIDS if you were so foolish and immoral as to engage in illicit sexual activity. You might as well play Russian roulette as practice "safe sex," said the ad. The only way to protect yourself from HIV is "abstinence before marriage, then marriage and mutual fidelity for life to an uninfected partner. Anything else is potentially suicidal."

At the time this ad appeared, there was increasing published evidence that consistent practice of so-called "safer sex" did in fact dramatically reduce rates of transmission of HIV. One would never have known this from reading the Focus on the Family ad, with its shrill insistence that "safe sex" was essentially the same as suicide, only slower. But I was familiar with the current epidemiological wisdom concerning HIV transmission, and I wondered: Why was it so important to the Focus on the Family writers to deny this? What would they lose if it were possible to prevent the transmission of HIV by, for example, the consistent use of condoms? And what exactly was the sexual morality that they were promoting? Was it merely incidental that they portrayed virginity and marital fidelity solely as disease-prevention strategies, or was this really at the center of their sexual ethic?

It seemed to me that there were a couple of complementary currents of thought running beneath the surface of this ad. One was a view of the world in which people get what they deserve. AIDS, so this train of thought goes, is a very bad thing. Anyone who has AIDS must have done something very bad to deserve it. Anyone who would risk exposure to AIDS must be similarly morally corrupt. Therefore, such persons deserve to get AIDS, too.

We might call this the "Job's comforters" approach to AIDS, or indeed to suffering of any kind. When Job was struck with suffering, three of his friends came, they said, to comfort him. This supposed comfort consisted in urging him to remember

117

and confess the sins he must have committed in order to deserve his sufferings. "Think now," says one of his friends. "Who that was innocent ever perished? Or where were the upright cut off?" In other words, it is impossible that this is not all your own fault. Repent! Then everything will be okay again.

In fact, as the narrator of the story makes clear in the beginning, Job's sufferings were never a result of his sin. Job's comforters were wrong when they assumed that great suffering is an infallible indicator of great sin. And yet, this assumption has proven powerfully attractive to legions of Job's comforters after the biblical ones. Suffering—especially the suffering of other people—seems so much more manageable if we assume it is those others' own fault. Suffering then also serves the handy purpose of flagging everyone who has been bad. Do you want to know who the sinners are? Just look for the sufferers.

But now imagine that it might be possible to sin and yet to escape suffering. Imagine, for example, that it were possible to have illicit sexual relations and yet not come down with a sexually-transmitted disease. How could anyone tell who the sinners were? It would be very confusing. More than that, it would turn the moral framework of the world upside down: it would make it possible for people to avoid reaping the consequences of their sin. Hence the horror of modern-day Job's comforters at the idea that it might be possible, through the practice of "safer sex," to prevent the transmission of HIV. Never mind that the sex in question might be perfectly licit by traditional Christian moral standards: for example, a wife having marital relations with her HIV-infected husband. Job's comforters, in their eagerness to maintain that people who go astray will certainly get what is coming to them, cannot be bothered to distinguish questions of epidemiology (How can HIV transmission be prevented?) from questions of Christian morality (What is morally good sex?). Epidemiology and morality are conflated: AIDS is bad, people with AIDS are bad, sex with people with AIDS is bad. Decent people should stay very far away from AIDS and people with AIDS, and then everything will be fine.

118

This is the flip side of the Job's-comforter approach to suffering: the idea that the Christian life is fundamentally an exercise in looking out for number one. Self-preservation is the highest of all goods, and the fundamental motivators of Christian moral behavior are therefore self-interest and fear. Thus the authors of the Focus on the Family ad dismiss all talk of "risk reduction," and make clear that, in their view, it is never enough simply to reduce one's risk for HIV; what is needed is the complete elimination of any risk. That is what virginity and marital fidelity are for: they are essential components of a comprehensive disease-prevention strategy. One wonders what other components of such a strategy might be. Christian physicians refusing to treat HIV-infected patients? Christian parents removing their children from schools attended by HIV-infected children? Christian churches barring their doors to HIV-infected people?

It is hard to reconcile this vision of the Christian life with Jesus' words: "Greater love has no man than this, that he lay down his life for his friends." Jesus seemed to think that a Christian person might be called to risk or even to give his or her life in the service of another. Did Jesus mean to make an exception for certain kinds of risks—nonrespectable ones like AIDS, for example? Given that Jesus went willingly to the most shameful death the ancient world had to offer, this seems unlikely.

It also seems unlikely that Jesus would recommend virginity and marriage in quite the same terms as Focus on the Family did, namely as "the only . . . safe way to remain healthy in the midst of a sexual revolution." According to Jesus, the whole of the Christian life can be summed up as the love of God and the love of neighbor. Shouldn't it rather be the case that Christians practice sexual purity and faithfulness because they are disciples of a pure and faithful God whom they love and wish to imitate? And shouldn't Christians respond mercifully to those who suffer, given the mercy Jesus showed to suffering people?

But love, either as a motivation to action or as the content of one's behavior, flies out the window rather quickly for many people, including many Christian people, when AIDS comes

119

into view. AIDS, after all, is a disease of bad people. Good people do not run risks that might result in their meeting a fate that strikes only bad people. Thus, for example, the president of a Christian college, upon finding out that I was married to a man with AIDS, telephoned me long-distance to berate me for my supposed naiveté in believing that condoms reduce the risk of transmission of HIV. He then rescinded the approval he had given that I be hired at his institution.

Where was love, as Christians confronted AIDS?

If living with AIDS gave Hyung Goo and me an uncomfortable perspective on Christian rhetoric concerning AIDS, being Christians gave us at least as uncomfortable a perspective on the internal rhetoric of AIDS. One of the things that people do when confronted with incomprehensible disaster is attempt to construct some sort of narrative that promises to make sense out of the suffering it details. This effort received extra impetus in the case of AIDS, because so many of those who suffered with AIDS in the early years of the epidemic were artists of various kinds: dancers, musicians, photographers, filmmakers. Sometimes it seemed that we could hardly turn around without coming up against some artistic expression or other that had AIDS as its subject. And yet, so many of these efforts to create meaningful narrative seemed to fall breathtakingly short, to do no more than call attention to the fact that the person who spoke through this creation had, in fact, no hope at all.

In the spring of 1993, the documentary film *Silverlake Life* was shown on public television. *Silverlake Life* was made by a gay filmmaker and his lover, both of whom had AIDS, as a sort of video diary of their life and (as it turned out) the filmmaker's death from AIDS. The film was essentially a love story, and, as such, it touched a lot of nerves in me. I found all too much in the film to identify with—the love, the anger, the fear, the helplessness, the companionship and devotion these two men had with and for each other. And there was all too much insight into the experience of the sicker partner, who died in the course of the film. He was tired, sick, frightened, hopeless; and, at the end, in so much pain, so disfigured by

120

disease that seemingly nothing was left of his humanity except his capacity to suffer.

There was a scene toward the end of the film in which Mark, the less sick partner, was filming Tom, who was lying in bed, eyes closed, close to death. Mark was weeping, and saying, "I fed Tom some food that didn't agree with him, and he was up all night vomiting. I shouldn't have done it. I felt so bad. I felt so guilty, so ashamed. I shouldn't have done that to him."

"Someday, that will be me," I thought. "I will feel just that way. I will have had just such an experience." I think there was a sense, in fact, in which I already felt this way—responsible in some major way for Hyung Goo's well-being, and yet utterly helpless to accomplish it, weeping somewhere inside myself in rage and frustration, and feeling myself accused somehow for not being able to control things that were completely beyond my control.

One would think that watching this film might have made me feel less alone, that it might have made me feel that there were others who had shared the experiences I had had and would have. In fact, this was not the effect. Faced with the film's bleak realism, I felt more isolated than ever. These two men, both of whom had experienced great alienation, had found a measure of solace in their love for one another; but their lives had devolved into a spiral of suffering and hopelessness in which there was, in the end, no meaning to be found. Their attempts to create some kind of significance for their lives—through their defiant affirmation of gay culture, through their films, through their dabblings in the supernatural—were pathetic, and obviously so. Tom said at one point, agitatedly, "I can't remember things anymore. I can't remember any of the good things I've done. It's the things you've done that give meaning to your life . . . isn't it?" It was obvious from the film exactly how much meaning his work gave to his life. He died, racked with pain and devoid of hope, leaving behind his lover, whose only comfort as he anticipated his own death was to imagine that he sensed Tom's disembodied spirit flitting about the room from time to time.

The alternative to these stark portrayals of the suffering of people with AIDS seemed most often to be a sort of black humor: attempts, mostly desperate, to make fun of the disease itself, its treatment regimens, the feelings evoked in people with AIDS or people at risk for AIDS. A cycle of songs, the AIDS Quilt Songbook, which was first performed in New York City in 1992, and which I heard in Durham in 1995, included a number of songs in the black humor category. "Fairy Book Lines," with its punning title, offered parodies of nursery rhymes: "Death be nimble—life was quick. . . . Poor old Charlie, he swallowed a fly; The fly was drunk with MAI. . . . Twinkle, twinkle, eyes in pain; Retinitis makes its awful gain. . . ." Each verse ended with death, through fever, pneumonia, suicide: "Now a bag slides over the head—too bad! So long to the world so long desired: darkness sucks you down its drain."

A song for baritone and clarinet, "The 80's Miracle Diet," gave advice on "how I lost 40 pounds in two weeks . . .", details available "free without the asking, Quick delivery by overnight male." Diet specifics are given: "Cocktails of Perrier with a twist of AZT, Bactrim broiled with bacon bits, Egg lipid quiche for brunch. . . ." Abruptly, the song breaks out in an anguished wail: "The most talented minds, the best bodies of my generation going up in smoke." Then the lyricist recovers his mocking, deadpan stance: "Act now. Dial 1-800-I-GOT-IT-2. Our operators are standing by. I have photographs to prove it: Before and After and Passed Away."

Most of these songs had a very hard time staying humorous. What they were talking about was terribly, unutterably sad. The songwriters and the performers alike knew that full well, but they didn't know what else to do. Neither did lots of other people. Hyung Goo and I had a friend whose sister and brother-in-law both died of AIDS during the course of our marriage. We knew of their illnesses, and heard of their deaths through mutual friends, but Rini seldom spoke of them to us, and never talked with us about our or her own experiences with AIDS. After Hyung Goo's death, Rini confessed to me that she had kept her distance from us because she had felt there was nothing she could say. She felt she would have had to be supportive, or make morbid jokes, or something, and she just couldn't. All she could have done was tell us how horrible it was, and even that would have been futile, because we would have to find out for ourselves.

Where was hope, in the world of AIDS?

A few months after Hyung Goo's death, I participated in a panel discussion at Duke Divinity School that was part of a continuing-education event designed to assist pastors in responding appropriately to AIDS. Among the other panelists were a retired minister whose son had died of AIDS, an HIV-positive black man, and an older man in the final stages of AIDS.

The minister said that his son, Paul, had stopped going to church when he was in college because (as his father found out much later) someone had told him that homosexuals had no place in the church. Paul didn't tell his family that he was gay or that he had AIDS until a year or so before his death. I heard later, from a social worker who had known them, that Paul's parents and siblings had responded to his illness with extraordinary love and compassion. But they kept the specifics of Paul's illness to themselves, and perhaps that was prudent, because when their church found out that Paul had died of AIDS, they were ostracized. They ended up leaving that church and going to another. Paul's father said, "The church let my son down, and it has let down everyone else who is gay."

Robert, the black man with HIV, talked about the particular challenges and isolation he experienced as a gay black man. He felt rejected by the black community, rejected by the church, and an outsider to the (mostly white) gay community. He served on the boards of a number of AIDS service agencies, but had kept his own HIV status a secret from most of his family members. Of the few relatives who knew, some had responded with rejection, others with only tentative acceptance. He had just that very day spoken with his pastor about being gay and having HIV. What would come of that? It was too soon to know.

Bill, the older man with AIDS, was the angriest of all. Everyone was hateful. His family wouldn't speak to him. He had had HIV for fifteen years, had been doing chemotherapy for many of those years, and was beginning to feel that his life was not worth living. Two hundred of his friends had died. He had been present at the deaths of six of them. He had heard of a church that had ruled it would not conduct funerals for suicides or persons with AIDS. This made him twice an outcast, as he planned to kill himself, possibly soon. "People who call themselves Christians should act like it," he said. "Jesus said, 'As you did it unto the least of these my brethren, you did it to me.' I am one of 'the least of these,' and I plan to tell God exactly what other Christians did or didn't do for me."

Then it was my turn. As the date of the meeting had approached, I had wondered what I should say. It had not occurred to me to wonder what the other panelists would say. Now I wondered why I had even come. What could I say, what could anyone say, in the face of such anger and hurt and alienation? Lacking any better option, I told the truth. I said that after years of keeping secrets, we told everyone we knew, and they all responded by taking care of us. Our church's intercessory prayer group prayed for us. The members of our small-group Bible study shared their lives with us. The women of the church gathered around me in my widowhood. And I told the story of Hyung Goo's and my marriage: how even in the midst of HIV and AIDS we had managed to get married and stay married and have a full and happy life together. Hyung Goo had lived and died well, and it had been an honor to be his wife.

When the meeting was over, we all stood to leave. I had been seated next to Robert. He turned to me and said, "May I hug you?" He embraced me and said, "You give me hope that someday I will find someone who will love me, even though I have HIV." The depth of the divide that his words crossed was vertigo-inducing: he was gay, black, male, HIV-positive; I was straight, white, female, HIV-negative. And yet, he saw the love that Hyung Goo and I had shared with one another and had received from those around us, and he reached out and found hope.

I would like to think it is significant that this connection took place, if not actually within the household of faith, then at least in its general vicinity. A divinity-school continuing-education forum is not the church, but everyone who was present was a pastor or a parishioner at some church congregation. When we left, we all went home to those congregations. Could love and hope return with us? Could faith, hope, and love come together to form a healing and unitive response to AIDS, in contrast to the existing rhetorics of AIDS, which seemed to allow only for recrimination and division?

# A GREEN AND DYING TREE

The question of healing came up repeatedly in our lives, especially after we began to tell people about Hyung Goo's illness. A lot of his relatives, in particular, thought that what you should do about AIDS was pray for healing. Hyung Goo wasn't quite sure how to respond to this. He would have liked nothing more than to be healed, and prayed himself for healing, but he wasn't sure he wanted to trail around to Korean Pentecostal faith healers, which seemed to be what his family members had in mind.

We broached the subject with the minister who had married us. Had he prayed with people for healing? Had he been invited to do so, or had he volunteered? What had happened as a result? David told us that he had been asked to pray with sick people for healing on various occasions. He had done so, and some had been healed and some hadn't. As he understood it, the initiative rested with the sick person—it was up to him or her to ask for such prayer, or not.

Hyung Goo found this enormously freeing. It made him feel that he was in charge of his own response to his illness. Other people could pray privately that he would be healed—that was fine and he welcomed it—but he could make his own decisions about whether to seek out formal prayer specifically for healing, and not feel that he was being delinquent if he didn't expend a lot of energy doing so.

By the fall of 1994, Hyung Goo had been seriously ill for a year. He had had pneumonia off and on since the spring, along with chronic anemia, nausea, pain, and the eye infection for which he was taking IV medication once or twice a day. In October I received a summons to jury duty in federal court. I wrote a letter requesting to be excused on the ground that there was serious illness in my family. Hyung Goo practically dictated the letter to me, and it came out sounding like he had one foot in the grave and the other on a banana peel. "These people aren't rocket scientists," he said. "You have to make it very clear that you have to be at home to take care of me."

I found it unsettling to realize that there were, in fact, many days when Hyung Goo would have found it very difficult to take care of himself, even if that were construed to mean nothing more than getting his own meals. It wasn't that he needed to be waited on hand and foot all the time; it was that he simply didn't have the energy to do the regular everyday things that most of us spend a lot of time doing, and that I had become accustomed, of necessity, to doing for both of us.

In that same autumn, Hyung Goo began to be more joyfully engaged with life than almost ever before. I noticed the change increasingly as Christmas approached. The year before, he had been exhausted and in pain from starting chemotherapy at too high a dose, and miserably depressed from having to leave work. The only reason Christmas happened at all was that I made it happen by sheer force of will. But the next year, Hyung Goo was eager to get the tree, to do the shopping, to send the cards. I arrived home one day to find that he had just written the Christmas letter—something I had had to beg and plead with him to do the previous year. And he started talking about wanting prayer for healing.

I found this very disconcerting. We had spent the previous eight months planning the funeral, meeting with the funeral director and ministers, buying a cemetery plot—and *now* we were going to pray for healing, now that we were ready for him to die? And how was it that, as his health continued to deteriorate, he could be so happy, at least at those times when he had enough energy to feel something other than tired? I spelled out my puzzlement to a friend over the telephone. "Well," said Allan, "we're all going to die. That means that any prayer for healing is essentially a prayer for more time. It makes sense that as Hyung Goo realizes how seriously ill he is, and how short his time may be, he would be specially in love with life, and would want more time."

It did make sense. Hyung Goo spoke with our pastors about his desire for healing prayer. They planned a service for a weekday night in February, and invited the elders of the church, the members of our Bible study group, and any others of our friends who wished to come.

The road Hyung Goo had traversed to that request was long and circuitous. His family had been Christians since soon after the arrival of Western missionaries in Korea. Hyung Goo's father was a pastor, and both his parents worked hard to instill Christian faith in their children. Hyung Goo went off to college considering himself a Christian, and became involved with the college-age group at Park Street Church. But as his life fell apart, so did his Christian faith. Much of his behavior was all too obviously at odds with his Christian confession. Increasingly it seemed to him that, far from being a source of strength and encouragement for living, God was a convenient scapegoat whom he blamed for the state of his life. Perhaps God's consistent failure to come through with the blessings he prayed for—deliverance from sin, spiritual joy to replace his deep unhappiness—was evidence that God did not exist after all. Perhaps it was time for him to start running his own life, rather than hoping for someone else to give him good things. "I needed to stop blaming God and others for my own misfortunes," Hyung Goo wrote in his memoir. "I was the only one who had the power to make my life into what I wanted it to be."

Never one to do things halfway, Hyung Goo stood up at a meeting of the college-age fellowship, announced his renunciation of the Christian faith, and walked out. He decided that reality was purely material, the result of countless random events. Since there was no God and no moral authority, he could do as he pleased, and bore full responsibility for his own life. For awhile, this seemed to work: he reenrolled in school, he did well in his classes, he terminated his psychotherapy. Then all the wheels fell off again. A failed relationship reactivated all his old insecurities. He found himself unable to do any work, and withdrew from school again, very late in the semester. "So much for my self-improvement program," Hyung Goo wrote. "Now my self-image was shattered."

His materialistic worldview was shattering, too. He met several people who claimed to be psychic, including a middle-aged taxi driver named Swifty whose spiritual pilgrimage was being directed, so he said, by Carl Jung and the ancient Egyptian architect Imhotep. Hyung Goo became persuaded that he was psychic, too, and set about reading all the books related to paranormal phenomena in the Cambridge Public Library. He studied with a psychic who encouraged him to develop a supposed gift for telepathic communication. He joined the Society for Human and Spiritual Understanding, a pseudo-church that met on Sunday mornings in a small sanctuary-style room to practice meditation and listen to the pronouncements of a trance medium through whom spoke the voice of an Egyptian priest who had lived 3500 years before.

"Through my involvement in the world of psychics," Hyung Goo wrote, "I began to notice a consistent world view all these people held. It was subjective and egocentric. The world had been created purely out of the imaginations of human beings. Gravity, the mass-energy equilibrium, trees and mountains, as well as pain and suffering, love, joy and hate existed because human beings had individually and collectively decided upon a world in which they were necessary. This being the case, so the reasoning went, humans also had complete power to influence and change both small and large details of their world. We had power over illness, life and death. If we thought correctly, we could be immortal, as well as find a better job, greater financial wealth, the ideal life partner, and so on. It was completely up to me.

"The good thing about such a world view," Hyung Goo observed, "is that it gives a certain sense of empowerment to people who feel generally disenfranchised. The power of positive thinking has been amply demonstrated. The more we act on the belief that we can influence the course of our lives, the more likely that things will turn out as we had hoped. Taken to its logical extreme, however, it seeks to make gods of us all; and when it runs up against the objective world outside our imaginations (being hit by a truck, for example) it is proven inaccurate and inadequate."

Now Hyung Goo was in a quandary. His materialistic view of the universe had been superseded by one that had a palpable spiritual dimension, and yet the world view of his fellow psychics appeared increasingly flawed. Then providence intervened. His family received a visit from some relatives who lived in England. Aunt Eun-ja and Uncle Charles were devoutly charismatic Christians who were horrified to hear of Hyung Goo's involvement in the world of psychics. Did he not realize, they asked, that this was in fact the realm of the occult? They provided him with several books that Hyung Goo read while his relatives spent two weeks traveling in other parts of the United States. By the time of their return, he had become persuaded of the truth of the gospel and his need of the good news it offered. At Easter of 1982, three years after he had walked out of church, he walked back in.

It was at Park Street Church that I met Hyung Goo. I had been brought up going to church, but had not been taught to believe. Eventually I realized this made no sense, and stopped going. When the college choirs of which I was a member sang for chapel services, I participated in the anthems (because that was performance) but refused to join in the hymns (because that was worship). Toward the end of my college career, however, I became less persuaded of the adequacy of a purely secular view of the world, and more persuaded that perhaps the Christian version of reality was the true one. Around Easter of 1982, I, too, came back to church.

A few years later, I moved to Boston, where I began attending Park Street because it was the only church in Boston I had heard of. I joined the post-college-age young people's group, and participated in their meetings and retreats. Hyung Goo had by now graduated to this group as well, and at one retreat we were members of the same discussion group. I retain a memory of him from that occasion, an image at once vivid and tiny, as if seen through the wrong end of a telescope: Hyung Goo, very slight and sober, talking quietly and deliberately about his father's absence from the family when he was young.

In Durham we ended up at Blacknall Memorial Presbyterian Church, a congregation that drew its membership largely from the academic and medical communities associated with Duke. About the only person in the church who knew how to fix a dishwasher was the pastor, who could often be found at congregants' homes doing just that. On the other hand, if you needed heart surgery, there were half a dozen surgeons to choose from, and one of them was probably a member of your Bible study group.

Our Bible study group included the inevitable doctor—a medical student, actually—along with a veterinarian, a house painter, an attorney, a secretary or two, a teacher, a dental student, a campus ministry staff person, an employee of the sewer department, and assorted mothers of young children. We had been placed deliberately in this group by one of the pastors of the church. We had explained our situation to him when we joined the church, and he thought of a group that he hoped could rise to the challenge of enfolding a couple like ourselves, who were going to be very needy in the years to come.

There were five or six other couples in the group, and one or two single people. Some of them had children and some of them didn't. None of them was particularly like us. They certainly weren't living with terminal illness, and most of them knew no one else who had AIDS. We learned together that you don't need to share another person's precise circumstances in order to be supportive. You need only a willingness to share your own life and to share the life of another. You need to want to know what is really going on, even if you have no idea what to do.

Hyung Goo's illness and death were not the only things happening in that Bible study group. In the time that we were members of it, there was a marriage, a divorce, the birth of a couple of children and the adoption of another, several hospitalizations, a couple of surgeries, along with all the everyday challenges of home and work and school. We talked and listened and cried and prayed through it all. In that group, Hyung Goo got to care for others, as well as be cared for by them; he got to share their lives, to play with their children, to be part of the family of the church.

As the date of the healing service drew near, both Hyung Goo and I wondered how we should approach it. Hyung Goo found himself caught between faith and doubt. He wrote to a friend, "I ask myself: Do I really believe that miraculous healing is possible? There is a skeptical side of me, and there is also the side that desperately wants to believe and hope." For me, the tension was between faith and anger. If God really desired our good, why hadn't he kept Hyung Goo well in the first place? And did I really want to ask for healing from a God who had already shown himself callous enough to let Hyung Goo get as sick as he'd already gotten?

And what would it mean to approach prayer for healing with "faith"? What exactly were we hoping for? For reversal of Hyung Goo's HIV status? For him to feel better? Live longer? Be affected in some more spiritual or personal way? Did we honestly believe that he could or would be healed? What would happen if we prayed for healing and no healing was granted? Would Hyung Goo lose heart and die sooner than he might have otherwise?

How ought one to pray for healing, anyway? Church historian David Steinmetz, lecturing in a class for which I was a teaching assistant, offered a description of the difference between conventional Protestant prayer and the psalmists' prayers. The Protestant prays, "O Lord, we're not worth much. We have these people we want you to heal. We don't think you'll do it. Thy will be done. Amen." The psalmist prays, "O Lord, remember the deuteronomic law code? It says you will vindicate the righteous. Well, I'm righteous, and I'm a little short in the vindication department. Hello? Hello? Is there anybody there?" The psalmist's prayer certainly seemed the more robustly faithful, but I wasn't sure I was up for such prayer.

Perhaps, we decided, what we could hope for, in the most basic sense, was good: that whatever happened, God still had good things for us. "After all," I wrote to a friend, "we've been married almost four years now, under circumstances that most people would think pretty lousy, and we have received wonderful gifts of companionship and love and comfort. So suppose we pray for healing and Hyung Goo's health continues to deteriorate at its present rate, or faster. Does this mean there can be no good for him, or for us, in the midst of this? I don't think so. But I'd rather he just got well."

The healing service was attended by thirty or forty people. All the members of our Bible study group were there, along with other friends from church and elsewhere and most of the elders of the church. Everyone prayed for him and for us. It was obvious what Hyung Goo's role in the event was: he was the reason we were all there. It was less obvious what my role was. Was I there to pray, or to be prayed for? That night I had a dream in which someone had died, and a crowd of people were praying around the casket while I looked on, not sure how much a part of the scene I should be.

That service of prayer for healing bore fruit in a variety of ways. Hyung Goo did not wake up the next morning without AIDS, and he took that as an indication that time really was short. That realization spurred him into doing some things that were important to him in the time he had left. He wrote down memories of his childhood and youth and adult life. He corresponded with friends. He listened to music. He talked with me about the years we had been married, thinking over the ground we had covered and rejoicing in it.

The service also brought together most of the friends and other church members who were to be important to us in the last months of Hyung Goo's life. We were used to thinking of our friends as people who lived elsewhere, as indeed all our friends of many years' standing did. We hardly realized how many friends we had gained during our few years' residence in Durham until we saw them all together at that healing service. Hyung Goo died about six months later, and that prayer service came to seem like the inaugural event of that final trajectory,

133

the point at which all these people came together to see us through to the end.

Most fundamentally, however, those prayers for healing took place in the midst of a work of healing that was already well underway. Bruce Cockburn sings, "Two thousand years and half a world away, dying trees still will grow greener when you pray." Even as Hyung Goo died, he quickened. In the weeks and months before the prayer service, I had begun to see it happening, and hardly knew what to think. Hyung Goo seemed to be undergoing the same sort of transformation that happens in sentimental Victorian novels when somebody dies young. It was as if he were glowing. Every time he looked at me, all I could see was how much he loved me, and it made me feel he was not long for this earth.

A friend mentioned in a letter that she had been reading Paul's words in 2 Corinthians: "We, who with unveiled faces all reflect the Lord's glory, are being transformed into his likeness with ever-increasing glory." Oh, I thought, with a start of recognition. Maybe that was what I was seeing when Hyung Goo looked at me and all I could see in his face was love. I was not succumbing to sentimental imagination. I was living with an icon, with a person whose face had begun to shine like Moses' did when he came down from the mountain.

The weirdly preternatural glow didn't last, or else I just got used to it. Either way, it was a relief. Experiencing Hyung Goo as if he had an aura around him had been awfully strange. But the transformation continued. I had always thought him a person of fine character, which seemed remarkable enough, given how screwed up and miserable he had been for much of his life. Increasingly, though, it seemed that Hyung Goo was at peace in a way he hadn't been when we met or when we first were married. And I could see that peace, and share in it, in part because the depression that had enveloped him to a greater or lesser extent for so much of his life had lifted. I had wondered sometimes if I would ever really know Hyung Goo apart from that depression and the way it muffled his voice and blurred his outline. Now, free from its smothering shroud, he was present and open, able to love and to be loved, even on days when he was exhausted and in pain and grieving over the losses he had suffered thus far and those yet to come.

In a way as undeniable as it was mysterious, Hyung Goo was more whole when he died than he had been at any other time in his life. It was not the sort of healing that we had hoped or asked for. How could we have asked for it, when we couldn't even imagine it? But it was real, more real than the shabby appearances that are so easy to mistake for reality, as real as new green leaves on a dying tree.

# APRIL 1, 1995: FOSCARNET

In March of 1995, Hyung Goo was diagnosed with a reactivation of the CMV infection in his right eye. His doctors put him back on a twice-a-day schedule of Ganciclovir, hoping that would halt the progress of the infection. When it didn't, they decided it was time to try a new drug, Foscarnet.

We were not happy about this development. We weren't happy that Hyung Goo's CMV was not responding to Ganciclovir, because every reactivation of the infection meant more loss of vision. We weren't happy that he had to start Foscarnet, because its potentially serious side effects required that patients be admitted to the hospital for observation when starting the drug, and we had hoped Hyung Goo would never have to be in the hospital for any reason. And we weren't happy about the complexity that Foscarnet would add to the medication routine even if Hyung Goo proved able to tolerate it. For the first two weeks it was administered, Foscarnet had to be taken three times a day with each dose preceded by 250 ml of saline. That meant an hour for the saline and an hour for the medication, every eight hours. And Hyung Goo had recently been rediagnosed with PCP and put back on IV Pentamidine. I wrote to a friend, "With the saline, the Foscarnet, and the Pentamidine taken together, we're looking at his having to spend eight hours out of every twenty-four hooked up to an IV. This is going to drive both of us around the bend."

Hyung Goo was admitted to the hospital on Saturday, April 1. He seemed to tolerate the medication well enough, and was discharged on Monday. On Tuesday morning, I went to school to attend a lecture. Hyung Goo hadn't been feeling very well when I left, so after class I called to find out how he was. "Come home immediately," he said. "You need to take me to the emergency room." I arrived home to find Hyung Goo shaking uncontrollably and vomiting into the kitchen sink. We drove to the emergency room, where he was diagnosed with hypocalcemia. As he lay on the gurney with a calcium drip hooked up to his Hickman line, the shaking subsided. What had this morning's lecture been about, he asked me. The English Reformation, I told him. Evidently he wanted to get his mind off his troubles, because he was not satisfied until I repeated to him everything I had learned that morning about the regency of Somerset and the first prayer book of Edward VI.

Hyung Goo was readmitted to the hospital, where his doctors spent several days tinkering with his Foscarnet dosage and with potassium, calcium, and magnesium supplements, trying to get his blood chemistry back as it ought to be. We both hated his being in the hospital. Hyung Goo felt bored and dehumanized and like he had no control over anything. I felt I had to be at the hospital constantly so I could know what was going on, which left me with no time in which to decompress and gather myself for the next stretch. The number of caregivers was overwhelming. The attending physicians were perpetually surrounded by herds of residents, interns, and medical students. A new nurse came on every twelve hours, with the scheduling arranged so you never saw the same nurse twice. I wrote to a friend, "Hyung Goo is miserable, I am miserable, everybody's miserable."

Hyung Goo started throwing up everything he ate. What was wrong? Did he need to substitute a new antinausea medication for the one he had been taking? Was it the IV Pentamidine? Was it a drug interaction? Was it a reaction to the Foscarnet? There did seem to be a problem with his kidney function. A renal fellow came by for a consult late in the week. "Hey, no problem," he said, leaning up against the wall. "I've seen lots of cases like this. Your kidneys will recover on their own in a couple of days."

By Sunday, Hyung Goo's doctors had pumped him full of twenty-five pounds of excess fluid in their efforts to restore the balance of his electrolytes. Finally they realized that none of that fluid was being excreted. His kidneys had completely ceased to function. The excess fluid was backing up into his lungs and threatening to suffocate him. When his lungs were at their wettest, I could hear them rattling from three feet away. He started to hallucinate, apparently from a combination of insufficient oxygenation of the blood (because of the fluid in the lungs) and an accumulation in the blood of toxic substances (like uremic acid) and drugs (like morphine) that were not being cleared by the kidneys.

The ID clinic physician on call came by Hyung Goo's hospital room. Hyung Goo needed to decide whether he wanted to undergo dialysis, she said. He asked what his options were. "Well," she said, "without dialysis I am not certain you will survive. But if you don't want dialysis we can give you morphine and make you comfortable and let you go."

Hyung Goo was horrified. He was not ready to go. Yes, he wanted dialysis. A temporary dialysis catheter was placed in his femoral artery, and after a first, brief dialysis, he was already feeling better on Sunday evening. As the crisis mounted, I had been much on the telephone with our pastor and with Dan. Dan had offered to come by the hospital and see us, and in the evening I called and asked him to come. When he arrived, friends from church were in the room with us. Dan stayed while we visited with them. One by one they left, until just the three of us remained.

Dan sat by the bed and asked Hyung Goo how he was feeling. Hyung Goo turned to him and talked and talked, the words just spilling out of him. He felt so trapped by the whole hospital experience. All the adverse developments left him stunned. Of all the scenarios he had imagined for how his health might fail, kidney failure was not among them, and it took him completely by surprise. He felt he had had a taste of what it might be like to feel that just staying alive had become too great a struggle; and yet because he was married he felt he had me to live for. He wondered whether perhaps I had made too great a sacrifice in marrying him, giving the best years of my life to one who was so needy and who would not be able to stay with me long into the future. He wondered what would become of me after his death. Would I marry again? Might I bear or adopt a child?

There was more to the conversation than I could remember. It all felt like a dream. After the extreme anxiety of the morning, some improvement later in the day, and comforting visits with friends came this long quiet conversation at night, as Dan's listening presence evoked all the words that Hyung Goo needed to say and that I needed to hear. When Dan left, long after visiting hours had ended, I walked with him to the elevator, for once feeling purely grateful to him.

I slept in Hyung Goo's hospital room with him that night and for several nights thereafter. I reclined in the chair by his bed as he hallucinated, talking about toasters and basketball and socks as his hands picked at the air. "There are no toasters," I murmured all night. "No basketballs; no socks. Put your hands down. Try to sleep."

The next day, after Hyung Goo had undergone a second round of dialysis, the renal fellow came by to see him again. Hyung Goo asked him a question, and the fellow looked at the floor and said, "I just don't know. I have no experience with patients as immunologically compromised as you. You'll have to ask your own doctor." In fact, even Hyung Goo's own physician was by this time being very circumspect. I wrote to a friend, "A large part of the problem is that John, who is an extremely competent and experienced man, has never treated anybody who had the same constellation of things wrong with him that Hyung Goo does. Most people who are this sick are dead. So he is having to learn on Hyung Goo."

Even as Hyung Goo began to draw back from the brink of death, it started to become clear how inadequately he was being cared for. I realized on Monday that he hadn't been bathed for days, not since he had become too sick to get out of bed. Evidently patients who could stand up were expected to bathe themselves in the room's private shower bath; patients who couldn't stand up were expected to lie in their beds and mold. I bathed him myself every day for the remainder of his hospital stay.

On Tuesday, after his third round of dialysis, Hyung Goo experienced some kind of adverse reaction that left him persuaded that he had almost died. We never knew just what had happened, because he had been left alone in the treatment room while the dialysis staff did other things. When he got back to his own room, he was nearly hysterical. Later that day, he started to vomit while lying on his back. I turned him on his side so he wouldn't choke to death. Then he bled through the dressing on his dialysis catheter. I went and found a nurse to change the dressing so he wouldn't bleed to death. By this time I was hysterical too. It was all too clear that if I let him out of my sight for a minute, he would die from sheer neglect. I spent the rest of Tuesday and a good portion of the day on Wednesday summoning hospital administrators to his room and dressing them up one side and down the other for the scandalous understaffing of their hospital.

On Thursday the renal fellow took out the dialysis catheter, donning mask and gloves and doing the procedure in Hyung Goo's room with me assisting, because I didn't want him taken anywhere else in the hospital. We went home the next day. Hyung Goo's kidneys were recovering at a rapid rate, and his doctor could see that if he stayed in the hospital one second longer we would both lose our sanity. He had lost ten pounds and was barely able to stand up, but we couldn't get out of there fast enough.

The Foscarnet fiasco would have been bad enough as an isolated incident. In fact, it was just the most acutely awful part of a continuously awful spring, with one thing going wrong after another for months on end. Hyung Goo was tired all the time. He was severely anemic, requiring three units of packed red blood cells every three weeks, despite the drug he was taking to boost his red cell count. He had pain in his arms and legs that was unresponsive to narcotics and kept him awake at night. Toward the end of January we got a metal frame to keep the bedclothes off his feet, hoping that would lessen the

APRIL 1, 1995: FOSCARNET

pain. It did, but it also made him feel as though his feet were hanging out in the middle of space. "How do the astronauts get any sleep?" he wondered.

In February, Hyung Goo started running fevers again. Was it a recurrence of pneumonia? There was no way to tell unless and until it got worse. It did get worse. John diagnosed PCP, and would have put Hyung Goo back on IV Pentamidine, but we were scheduled to fly to the West Coast in a week to attend my brother's wedding, and IV Pentamidine was not a drug one could travel with. Hyung Goo went on Mepron instead—it wasn't as effective as Pentamidine, but it was portable and would, we hoped, keep the PCP in check for a couple of weeks until we got home. "You should see the amount of medicine and medical paraphernalia we travel with," I wrote to a friend as we were packing. IV tubing and supplies, syringes for injectable drugs, a doctor's note so he could carry the syringes onto the plane, a cooler full of IV and injectable medication, innumerable bottles of pills. It was a wonder there was any room for our clothes.

Hyung Goo was still running fevers when we returned. Perhaps they weren't due to PCP after all. Maybe it was something else. A few days later, he was diagnosed with a recurrence of CMV. Was that the source of the fevers? He went back on an induction dose of Ganciclovir. A few days after that, a culture came back positive for MAC (*Mycobacterium avium* complex), another common opportunistic infection. Here was another possible source of fever. Hyung Goo's doctor discontinued his PCP drugs and started him on MAC drugs. "It is not good that Hyung Goo has MAC," Martha said to me during one of my visits to the clinic. "People can live a long time with MAC, but such people generally don't have all the other things wrong with them that Hyung Goo does." That Sunday Hyung Goo felt very unwell, but got up and came to church anyway. A friend whom we hadn't seen in awhile came over to speak with us, took one look at Hyung Goo, and burst into tears.

The next day, I traveled to a job interview: two days of meetings, presentations, and working lunches and dinners, all involving large groups of complete strangers. "How are you

141

doing?" the chairman of the search committee asked toward the end of the second day. I started to cry. "I lead a very quiet life," I sobbed, idiotically. "All I do is keep house and go for walks. This is just too many people." He cancelled my next engagement and sent me off by myself for a few hours to regroup.

The day after I returned from the interview, Hyung Goo went to the clinic complaining of chest pain. An x-ray showed a partially collapsed lung, presumably the result of recurrent PCP. "So he is back on IV Pentamidine for that," I wrote to a friend. "This is the drug that makes him throw up for weeks. He would be in the hospital, were it not for the fact that his doctor trusts him, and us, enough to send him home with instructions to go straight to the emergency room should he experience symptoms suggesting the lung is collapsing further." An x-ray a week later showed that the lung collapse had reversed itself. An eye exam the same day indicated that his CMV was not responding to the increased dose of Ganciclovir. The next day Hyung Goo entered the hospital and the Foscarnet disaster began.

When Hyung Goo emerged from the hospital two weeks later, he went back on IV Ganciclovir, for whatever good it was still doing in suppressing the systemic effects of CMV infection. Where his vision in particular was concerned, the only treatment option remaining was an experimental procedure in which a time-release capsule of Ganciclovir was implanted in the eye, where it delivered medication directly to the retina. The procedure was still in clinical trials, but was available on a compassionate-use basis to patients who had been unsuccessfully treated with other therapies. Hyung Goo's doctors arranged for him to be seen at the Emory retina clinic, one of the sites where the procedure was done. The following Sunday we flew to Atlanta. We spent Monday at Emory being seen by the physician and having the surgery, and then had a followup visit on Tuesday morning. We flew home on Tuesday afternoon equipped with three different kinds of eyedrops: an antibiotic (to prevent infection), a steroid (to reduce inflammation), and a dilating drop (to keep the muscles of the eye relaxed while it healed). They were all painful. It was my job to administer them, as often as every hour.

A week later, Hyung Goo was diagnosed with an ulcer, undoubtedly the result of all the medication he was taking. The next week, he had another collapsed lung. The week after that, a detached retina, and surgery to repair it. And then, finally, unaccountably, things settled down. His eye healed. His abdominal pain lessened. His collapsed lung reinflated. His fevers, which had been spiking to around 103.5° every day for months, abated. It was the end of May. The spring from hell was over.

We made a couple of decisions in the course of the Foscarnet episode. For a long time the only people at church who had known of Hyung Goo's illness were the pastors and elders and the members of our Bible study group. We decided during Hyung Goo's hospitalization that it was time for the whole church to know what was going on. We asked our pastor to announce in church on Sunday, as a congregational concern, that Hyung Goo was in the hospital with kidney failure as a complication of AIDS.

The responses were basically of two kinds. A few people whom we hadn't known well to that point stepped forward and became persons of real significance in our lives. They visited at the hospital, entertained us in their homes later on, and joined with our other friends in their efforts to care for us. The majority of the congregation remained in the background. Many of them spoke to me at church the first time I was there after this announcement was made, telling me of their shock and sadness at hearing that Hyung Goo was ill. For the most part, however, they did not attempt to become visible presences in our lives. This was a good thing, in fact. We couldn't have dealt with a lot of new people at that point in our lives, and they realized that. One woman told me later that she had wanted to have us over for dinner sometime the summer before Hyung Goo died, but, she said, "What you had together just seemed too holy; I didn't want to barge in on that." She had seen that our horizons were closing down; it was too late for anyone else to come in.

143

What she could do, and what she and many others did, was pray for us. One night that summer I dreamt that Hyung Goo and I were making our way through a building with long corridors and lots of doors, but with little sense of where we were going or how to get there. We ended up gathered with a little group of people, singing some sort of liturgical chant from a text posted on the wall. Somehow we knew that everyone in the building was doing this simultaneously, although we couldn't see or hear more than our few companions because there were so many twists and turns in the corridors. The dream seemed to express my sense of all the unknown, unseen people who were praying with us and for us. In the fall and winter, after Hyung Goo's death, one person after another came up to me to ask how I was doing and to say, "I've been praying for you." It seemed at those times as if the faces of all those hidden prayers were becoming visible.

We also decided, in the wake of the Foscarnet experience, that we never wanted Hyung Goo to be in the hospital again. It was a far greater strain on both of us for me to nurse him at the hospital, where it was noisy and there was no edible food and we had constantly to be defending him against hordes of incompetent aides, overworked nurses, and cocksure doctors, than it was for me to nurse him at home, where the setting was familiar and comfortable and we didn't have to fight for control. "If Hyung Goo doesn't want to be in the hospital again, he doesn't have to be," Martha told us. "There aren't many things that can't be done at home if you're really determined to be at home."

# THE GARDENS

Duke University is home to a beautiful arboretum, the Sarah Duke Gardens. Hyung Goo and I spent some of our happiest hours there. We walked in the gardens weekly while Hyung Goo was still working, and daily after he retired from his job. We got to know the garden as if it were our own. It became an extension of our life together, its geography mirroring the geography of our lives.

One winter day, a few years after Hyung Goo's death, I was in Durham, having traveled there to attend a friend's vocal recital. It was the first week of February, not an auspicious time for a garden. I doubted that anything would be in bloom, but I couldn't be in Durham and not go to the gardens. As I set out on what had been Hyung Goo's and my usual route, I began to notice the winter textures and colors of the garden. I will content myself with these, I thought: the waxy blue berries and matte green foliage of junipers, the glossy green leaves of hollies, the branches and bark of a mockernut tree. Fat furry buds studded the branches of the Asian magnolias. A few flowers were open; one tree was covered with white stars with floppy petals. Another, I knew, would have enormous pink and white blooms; others, hand-shaped purple blossoms.

A new tree had been planted by the magnolias, a weeping Japanese apricot. Its flowers were like those of the upright Japanese apricots on the other side of the pond, borne on stubby stems along woody branches. We always called these trees Korean plums. "Everything the Japanese have, they stole from the Koreans," Hyung Goo would say, darkly. Their scent is

145

carried on the wind; you can smell them from fifteen feet away. And yet, the smell is delicate and elusive; you want to bury your nose in a blossom and drink it in. The pink blossoms smell of cinnamon; the white blossoms of banana. Their petals flutter to the ground in the breeze. You have to close your eyes when you smell them, so you don't get a twig in the eye.

The camellias had grown so much taller since we first started walking in the gardens. They towered over me. Our favorite one, with perfectly simple pure white blooms, was covered with buds but had no flowers open yet. Other camellias were already blooming: light pink, dark pink, some with great clusters of yellow stamens. Forsythia was in bloom, and witch hazel. A viburnum was covered with clusters of small waxy flowers, deep pink in the bud and pale pink within. Along the path by the pond were the skeletons of last summer's hibiscus—long stalks with husks of blossoms. Shimmering outlines of the fullness of last summer's green foliage and pink flowers seemed to hang about these dry remains, a promise of next summer's bloom.

As I came around the curve at the end of the pond, I saw that Lenten rose was blooming, its purple bells nodding amid rosettes of long slim leaves. The beech tree had kept its dry copper-colored leaves through the winter; they rustled in the wind. A Japanese hornbeam stood, a graceful oval, beside the stream. Next to it was a river birch, its twin trunks covered with peeling bark. Near it was another new tree, a weeping pussy willow, with glossy brown buds and furry catkins. At its foot bloomed a few clumps of the very earliest daffodils, the ones that look like dragons, with long yellow trumpets and swept-back coronas.

In the terraced gardens, pansies bloomed with tulips coming up in between. The big saucer magnolias bloom from the top down, and not until later in the spring, but one bud was coming out already, down below. Near it was the Russian tea olive, which blooms in the fall, with tiny orange blossoms and a heavy, sweet scent. Everywhere were clusters of green spikes, some with nodding buds already, a few with flowers already open.

How could the gardens be so full of bloom in the middle of winter? During Hyung Goo's and my marriage, I had dreams in which the beginnings and ends of things were oddly commingled: days that were dark and light at the same time, a parade that was either for Memorial Day or Labor Day but I wasn't sure which, seasons that were winter and spring simultaneously. As I walked in the garden, it was as if one of these dreams had come to life, as if all times were simultaneously present. I found myself wishing I could be there a week later, two weeks later. So many more things would be in bloom. But could I stand such fullness? It was enough. And yet, I longed for more.

Even so had Hyung Goo's and my marriage been—suffused by such a longing for more, even as we were acutely conscious of being happier almost than we could stand. I found myself unexpectedly transported back to the happiness of that time, of our life together, to the quality of experience that that life had—happiness welling up from deep within, overflowing the banks, so circumscribed, like the gardens themselves, and yet so deep and detailed and full of specific beauties—blossoms, colors, shapes, buds swelling and opening and fading, to be succeeded by later blossoms and then renewed in the new year. So much to notice, so much to enjoy, a fullness that is beyond expression.

The Duke gardens were established in 1939 by a gift from a granddaughter of the founder of Duke University. Many modifications to the original design were made over the years, but funding was haphazard and piecemeal. In 1990, a full-time development officer was hired for the gardens. As money began to be raised for the gardens, more of the garden's fifty-five acres began to be developed. Hardly a month went by without some new addition, whether of plants or landscape features—new perennial beds, an arched footbridge, a Japanese snow-viewing lantern, a polished wooden bench. Hyung Goo and I supervised construction on our daily visits.

We followed a regular route through the gardens, designed to take us past every blooming plant. We walked down the linden path to the formal rose garden, into the Asiatic Arboretum, through the plantings of camellias to the zigzag Japanese footbridge, around the pond with its plantings of Japanese iris, down the hill to the dawn redwood and past it to the terraces. At the terraces, we would walk by every bed and watch the flowers unfold, from the daffodils and tulips of spring through summer annuals to fall chrysanthemums. Then to the round lawn, the shrub roses, the azalea court, the long perennial beds leading back to the formal rose garden, and up the linden path to the garden gate.

A series of ponds had been built in the gardens over the years. At the foot of the terraces was a pond filled with goldfish. Waterlilies grew here, pink and yellow and blue. Sometimes a dozen would be in bloom at one time. Frogs lived between the rocks on the pond walls; children fished for tadpoles. Drainage problems used to cause this pond to flood periodically. When the water receded, the goldfish would be left stranded, gasping, on the flagstone terrace surrounding the pond. Eventually a larger pond was built nearby to control the runoff.

The larger pond was populated by a wide variety of ducks, including a number of nonnative ducks. We never knew who had put them there, but someone certainly had, because the wings of the nonnative species were clipped. One pair were small, brightly colored, exotically marked, with wings that stuck up like sails. We asked a passerby what kind of ducks they were, and were told they were quail. They weren't; they were Mandarin ducks, as we later learned. We named them Danny and Marilyn (Quayle), in memory of our erroneous informant.

We named all the ducks. A pair of wood ducks became Napoleon and Josephine: Napoleon for the crest that was reminiscent of an admiral's hat, and Josephine his consort. Pinko took his name from his pink bill; Paleface, from the white stripe across his head. Pinko and Paleface were best friends; they were almost always together. Two Asian shelducks, big yellowish ducks with bad tempers, we called the bullies, for their habit of biting the other ducks. A cinnamon teal was Rufus, for his color. A green-winged teal, a hooded merganser, pairs of redheads and pintails and northern shovellers all had to be content with being called according to their species.

The mallards were all Mr. or Mrs. Mallard. They were the only ducks that ever had ducklings, and some years there were many ducklings indeed. We counted one family of sixteen. A few days later, their number was greatly reduced. We could only suppose that there were foxes as well as ducks living in the gardens. We took bread with us every day to the gardens; our habits were so regular that the ducks began to see us coming and would flock to us to be fed. We would try not to feed the bullies, but our efforts at social control were never very successful.

The last spring of Hyung Goo's life was breathtakingly beautiful. A friend who had lived in central North Carolina for all of her childhood and much of her adult life said it was the most beautiful spring she could remember. From early February until May, every day was just a tiny bit warmer than the one before, so that spring unfolded in a perfect crescendo of bloom. Every day, we noticed flowers that just the day before had been in bud and were now open; every day the fabric of the garden came more alive.

In the Asiatic Arboretum, early daffodils were succeeded by magnolias, then by the interlaced pattern of dogwood and, redbud, and the high delicate canopy of crabapple and cherry. In the terraced garden, clumps of narcissus and hyacinths were followed by sweeping arcs of tulips, the pom-pom-like blossoms of Japanese cherries, waterfalls of weeping cherries, the great mass of wisteria on the pergola.

Azaleas bloomed everywhere; first tiny red ones, then purple and peach and white and pink, more shades of pink than can be named, wave after wave of bloom unfolding, seemingly without end. Hyung Goo was in the hospital for the first two weeks of April, at the peak of the azaleas. When he was released, too weak to walk, we borrowed a wheelchair and went straight to the gardens and sat among the azaleas.

The entire spring seemed as if it were a gift just for us. As one medical crisis succeeded another, the life of the garden surrounded us, buoyed us, filled us. Every day our life was beautiful as we walked in the garden. As spring grew into summer, and Hyung Goo's health stabilized, the garden mirrored our relief, the riotous beauty of spring giving way to the calmer beauty of summer. Rhododendrons and Japanese iris were followed by daylilies, ginger lilies, stargazer lilies. The beds of tulips were replaced by beds of annuals—blue forget-me-nots, pink and red and white dianthus, moss roses, cleome. Clumps of purple coneflower and black-eyed Susans bloomed along the paths.

Hyung Goo died that fall. The first time I went to the gardens after he died, I didn't know what to do with my hands. We had always held hands as we walked. How could I walk with no one holding my hand? I began to take my lunch to the gardens. Hyung Goo and I had seldom picnicked. "Why sit outside on the hard ground, when you could eat comfortably at the table and then take a walk afterwards?" Hyung Goo would ask. But I couldn't eat comfortably at the table. I could hardly eat at all. I would take my lunch and sit on a rock by the pond and eat as the leaves fell from the trees.

The next spring was as bleak as the spring before had been lush. There were ice storms in January, snow in February, and a couple of hard freezes in early March. The largest of the Asian magnolias had just started to bloom, and its dead, black blossoms draped over its branches like so many decaying banana peels. Flowers and trees bloomed out of order, or not at all, as the weather shifted from warm to cold, and buds froze on frosty nights too late in the season. The pansies kept getting killed; the wisteria didn't bloom at all.

The garden looked as bleak as I felt. It seemed grimly satisfying—why shouldn't the whole world be dead, while Hyung Goo was dead? Still, eventually there was bloom—too much bloom, as it turned out, for me. The brightness of the flowers was more than I could bear. I forsook Hyung Goo's and my usual route through the gardens, and began instead to walk in the garden of native plants. Hyung Goo and I hadn't walked here much because, we felt, there wasn't much to see. Flowers were few and subdued; the green and brown of trees predominated.

150

Now, the shapes and textures of leaves and bark were as much as I could take; the brightness of flowers was too much. I bought a field guide, and started learning trees: hornbeam, sweet gum, sassafras, catalpa. I had grown up in the Midwest. We had oaks, maples, elms. We didn't have these trees. They seemed exotic, alluring. One day I noticed trees with reddish round blossoms in clusters. False mimosa, the tree book said. And everywhere the loblolly pines that are so characteristic of North Carolina.

I had a conversation with the gardens development officer about what to do with all the memorial gifts that had been given in memory of Hyung Goo. The chief gardener led me through the gardens, discussing various projects he had in mind. One involved establishing a collection of species roses in an as-yet-undeveloped section of the gardens. The gardens already had a large formal rose garden, full of hybrid teas, but for all their beauty, we had always found them unsatisfying because they had hardly any smell. "What good is a rose that doesn't smell like a rose?" Hyung Goo would ask.

Our favorite rose was the Rosa rugosa, an untidy-looking shrub with heavily scented deep pink blooms. We would smell every single one of them as they opened through the summer, sometimes not being quite careful enough to check for bees first. I decided that a garden full of species roses would be just the thing to spend Hyung Goo's memorial money on. The plants went in that spring; a few years later they were three times the size they had been when they were planted.

As I walked around the lawn that February day, I saw the atlas cedar that had been uprooted in a hurricane a year or two previously. Its branches are thin and furry, like wires dipped in flocking. When I first saw it after the hurricane, it was tilted at a 45-degree angle, its root ball half out of the ground. I supposed it would die. But it had been righted and staked and had grown to twice its former size.

The whole garden seemed to be quivering with life. Among the terraces, signs said "Hosta," "Hemerocallis," "Paeonia." Where peonies were promised, there were only the dead stumps

151

of last year's stalks; where day lilies were promised, there were unprepossessing tufts of foliage; where hostas were promised, there was nothing at all. And yet I knew what lushness lay below the surface; those beds that were so brown and empty and, to the unknowing eye, so unpromising, would be full to bursting in a matter of months.

Is the whole world like this? Is this what it might be like to live in expectation, real expectation, of the resurrection? If I really knew what the new creation would look like, if I knew and expected it in the same fineness and specificity of detail as I expect hostas and peonies and daylilies in the garden, might I not look at the world and see, not something that is brown and unpromising and passing away, but the quivering of new life under the surface, ready to break forth in inexpressible beauty and fullness, just given time?

Was not Hyung Goo's and my life together like this? Empty and sere, and yet a seedbed of fullness and life for both of us. He died, and I was widowed; yet in his dying, we both were made alive. Hyung Goo, who had been so sad all of his life, and whose sadness deepened and intensified with his illness, nonetheless emerged in the last few years of his life from the depression that had dogged him all his life, into the joy of loving well and being loved. And with him I, too, found joy.

As I left the gardens, I encountered two old acquaintances, Ava and Jim. Ava had been one of Hyung Goo's colleagues at the university medical center laboratory where he worked. We hadn't seen each other in years, not since Hyung Goo was working. We had an awkward conversation, although the encounter was most welcome. I was glad to see them, and they me, but we had not much to talk about. We never really knew each other, and it was a long time ago.

I told them that I had remarried, finished my degree, moved to another state and become a college professor. Ava had long since finished her Ph.D. and was working on a postdoc. Jim was working for a biotech research firm in the Research Triangle Park that was developing a promising new drug for HIV. "Yes," I said. "There are so many changes in AIDS treatment since Hyung Goo's time. It is a different world now." I told them that walking in the gardens had brought back many memories. Hyung Goo was a good man, and we had a good life together. We wished each other well, and parted.

After I had gone a little way, they turned back to me and Jim called out, "We hope the rest of your life will be as happy as your life is right now."

Was I happier that day than I had been during Hyung Goo's and my life together? I was differently happy; the memories of that former happiness shimmered in the air—elusive, palpable, heartbreaking.

# DIVING

Toward the end of May of 1995, I dreamt that I was in a submarine, in a little, boxy room—perhaps the pilot house, since it had a compass and a wheel to steer with, but it didn't seem to have any windows. I was watching the compass and steering. The submarine kept veering off course; each time it did so, I steered the other way, to compensate. Suddenly the compass began spinning wildly. The ship was out of control, spinning, diving. There was nothing I could do. The compartment I was in tumbled violently about, and I with it. I fully expected to die, and composed myself to do so. I seemed to be unconscious for awhile. When I came to, all was still. I emerged from the little room and found myself walking long distances through dark streets, wearing shoes but no socks and in danger of getting blisters.

It seemed a pretty transparent dream—me trying to stay on course through all of Hyung Goo's illness, not being able to see where I was going, things spinning out of control despite my best efforts to the contrary. The final scene was one of great desolation—empty, quiet, cold, snowy. Coping with AIDS was a desolate experience. It cast a pall over our entire life, as we anticipated Hyung Goo's death, and with it the end of all the good we had experienced together.

154

"And you don't anticipate positive relationships in the future?" Dan asked, when I told him about the dream. I was immediately angry. There seemed to be all kinds of mental gymnastics required of me in order to cope. I wasn't supposed to think about all the terrible things that could happen, because that would make me anxious; I was just supposed to concentrate on the moment. But when I was thinking of losing what I was enjoying in the present, I was supposed to think ahead to possibilities of future relationships, as if that would make it not so bad to lose this one.

But it was not possible to think ahead in one sense (the positive) and not in another (the negative). And no, I didn't anticipate "positive relationships" in the future. It seemed to me that the intimacy that Hyung Goo and I had achieved in our few years of marriage was surely a once-in-a-lifetime experience. That intimacy was something we had now, and when it was over, it would be over. All I would be left with was a giant emptiness, like the dark and empty streets of my dream, like the dark and cold depths of the ocean surrounding a sunken submarine.

# SEPTEMBER 4, 1995:
# HOSPITALIZATION

Fever is a constant accompaniment of end-stage AIDS. For much of the summer of 1995, Hyung Goo was able to keep his temperature down by taking Tylenol around the clock. As August drew to a close, his fevers got worse. They broke through the Tylenol. They spiked high, at strange times, like in the middle of the night. Hyung Goo went in to the clinic on a Tuesday, where a chest x-ray showed pneumonia in both lungs.

Hyung Goo's regular doctor, John Bartlett, had been out of the country all summer. Dr. Hicks, whom Hyung Goo had been seeing in John's absence, was not in the clinic that day. Hyung Goo was seen by a physician neither of us had met before. Several times it seemed as if their conversation were coming to an end, and the doctor would begin to rise to leave. Each time Hyung Goo said, in his characteristically deliberate manner, "Now, I have another question . . . ," and she had to sit back down. I thought, "This woman has not yet had the Hyung Goo experience!"

Hyung Goo was already on medication for PCP. The doctor's opinion was that this pneumonia was therefore probably something else, and thus unlikely to get precipitously worse once treatment was begun. He was still plenty sick enough to be in the hospital, but since we were opposed in principle to his being hospitalized, she prescribed an antibiotic and sent him home.

Over the next few days it didn't seem that the pneumonia was getting worse, but the structure of our lives seemed to dissolve. We couldn't seem to get to bed before three in the morning. Hyung Goo couldn't focus on the most routine tasks, like getting dressed. The fall semester began that week. I was teaching an ethics class in the undergraduate department of religion. I came home from school one day to find Hyung Goo still eating his breakfast in his pajamas at four in the afternoon. "What if he dies right in the middle of the semester?" I thought. "What will I do?"

My anxiety drove Hyung Goo crazy. I hovered over him one morning until finally he said, "You know, sometimes you are just like a mother hen."

"I'm sorry," I said. "I'm worried about you."

"I know you are," he said. "Now stop it."

Dan, who had long been pushing for me to take antianxiety medication, started pushing harder. I was now seeing him twice a week, and still spent as much time sniping at him as opening up to him. Maybe, he suggested, I would be able to relax more in therapy—and thus benefit more from it—if I were to lie down on the couch, with him out of sight, à lá Sigmund Freud. "I think that would make me feel like a lunatic," I said.

"You feel like a lunatic already," he said. "It probably wouldn't be worse, and it might be better."

Hyung Goo's health worsened over the weekend. His fever on Saturday night was 104.7°. He was short of breath. By Sunday evening, we were frightened. But Monday was Labor Day, and the clinic was closed. We knew that going to the emergency room would mean being admitted to the hospital. "If we can just make it until Tuesday, " we thought, "we can go in to the clinic and be treated there."

On Monday morning, we woke up before dawn. Hyung Goo could barely breathe. He sounded like a freight train. He was disoriented and panicky—both consequences of oxygen deprivation, I realized later. He was in no condition to participate in a decision to go to the hospital, and somehow I couldn't come to that obvious conclusion on my own. I paged the ID clinic physician on call. It happened to be Dr. Hicks. "Go to the emergency room!" he said.

But how to get there? Hyung Goo could hardly walk. I couldn't get him into the car by myself. Hyung Goo would have been appalled at the idea of spending good insurance money on an ambulance. I called a friend, the veterinarian from our Bible study group. He was at our house within minutes. He half-carried Hyung Goo down the stairs, bundled him into his station wagon, and drove us both to the emergency room.

Dr. Hicks arrived soon after we did. "It must be PCP after all," he said, after blood work and an x-ray. By this time, Hyung Goo was lying on a gurney, breathing oxygen through a mask. As his oxygen levels rose, his breathing became less labored and his panic subsided. Dr. Hicks laid out his treatment options for him. "We can treat your PCP and give you oxygen through a mask and see if you get better. Or, we can treat your PCP and put you on a ventilator to assist your breathing, and see if you get better." Either way, we would know within a couple of weeks if it had worked—if patients this sick with PCP recovered, they usually did so within that time frame.

Did we want Hyung Goo put on a ventilator? The use of a ventilator was so contrary to all the ideas we had ever had about how we wanted Hyung Goo treated that we were startled when confronted with the decision of whether or not to use one. It seemed almost assured that he would die from this round of PCP if we refused the ventilator, and entirely possible that he would die even if we consented to it. But in Dr. Hicks' judgment, there was a reasonable possibility that with the ventilator Hyung Goo could push through this bout of PCP, and have a little more time. Did he want to give it a try?

A nurse stuck her head into the treatment room. "You have a visitor," she said. It was an elder from our church, himself an infectious diseases physician, albeit more involved in research than in patient care. Dr. Hicks left to care for other patients while we mulled over the idea of the ventilator. Rich stayed to answer all of Hyung Goo's usual questions. If he were on a ventilator, would he be conscious? Yes, although he would be under some level of sedation. Would it be painful? It would be uncomfortable, but the sedation and painkillers should make it tolerable. Would he be able to talk? No, but he might be able to communicate by writing little notes. I was feeling faint from stress and lack of food. An orderly brought me a bowl of Cheerios, and I ate them while Rich and Hyung Goo conferred.

Hyung Goo decided to give the ventilator a try. He was whisked off to another room to be sedated and have the tube placed in his trachea. A social worker accompanied me to a waiting room. When the tube was down, I was allowed in to see him. As I approached the gurney, he sat up and pulled the tube out. He hadn't been sufficiently sedated, no doubt because of the high tolerance of narcotics that he had developed over a year of taking morphine every day. As they saw him sit up and reach for the tube, all the respiratory technicians jumped on him at once. It seemed like there were half a dozen of them, pinning him to the table, holding his arms, getting the tube back into place, administering more sedative. I shrank back against the wall in tears. "He won't remember any of this!" one of the technicians called out over his shoulder. "I certainly will," I thought.

With the tube back in place, Hyung Goo was wheeled out of the room and onto the elevator to be admitted to the Medical Intensive Care Unit on the eighth floor of Duke North Hospital. I tottered out of the room after him, feeling completely traumatized. "There you are!" said the social worker, who had assumed I had fled the room while Hyung Goo was being worked on, and had been looking everywhere for me.

It took a while for Hyung Goo to be admitted to the MICU, in part because of all the additional tubes that needed to be placed: nasogastric (feeding) tube, urinary catheter, a catheter in his wrist so that his arterial blood gases could be monitored, a catheter in his neck for administering medication. I floated between the waiting room and the cafeteria for the several hours the procedures took. Dan came by the hospital in the afternoon, just as I was told I could go in to see Hyung Goo. We went in together. Another visitor was already there. "I had to tell them I was a clergyman to get in here," he said to me.

A weirdly formal moment ensued: "Dan, this is Dennis Campbell, Dean of Duke Divinity School. Dean Campbell, this is Dan Grandstaff, my psychotherapist." As these two avatars of my public and private lives shook hands, I half expected to see them both disappear, like matter and antimatter colliding.

Hyung Goo lay unconscious during the introductions. He had evidently been thoroughly sedated this time around. As long as he was asleep, I decided that maybe I had better get some sleep too. We had been dropped off at the emergency room in the morning, so I didn't have a car with me. Dan drove me home.

Hyung Goo and I had begun the summer with a two-week trip to Boston to attend his fifteenth college reunion. The trip was like a replay of our two months in Boston the previous summer, only on fast-forward, as we tried to see everyone and do everything, one last time. We had meals or conversations with half a dozen friends and relatives, and arranged an open-house party that was attended by many others. We went to the reunion and had innumerable conversations with old friends and complete strangers. We spent a weekend on Cape Cod with my family. We saw more friends in New York; we visited the Immigration Museum at Ellis Island; we went up the Empire State Building at dusk and watched the lights of the city come on. We ate our way from one end of the Northeast to the other: fried clams on Boston's North Shore, dim sum in Boston's Chinatown, boiled lobsters and steamer clams on the Cape, Korean food at our favorite restaurant in New York two nights in a row.

Unsurprisingly, we wore ourselves out. The morning we were to leave New York, Hyung Goo was so weak he had to rest for two hours before we could pack the car. We had lunch in New Jersey with Hyung Goo's sister and her husband. Hyung Goo sat and stared at the table, too exhausted to talk. When we left, he wanted to drive. I objected: he was too tired. It wouldn't be safe. He insisted. I was furious. As he drove along, listening to some late Beethoven string quartets, he started to cry. He was weeping; I was fuming; the traffic on the New Jersey Turnpike was swirling around us. Somehow we made it home. A week or so later I told Martha the story. Her one-word response: "Aaaahhhhh!"

This word might have served well to describe the entire summer. It was all too clear that the end was closing in on us, and yet it was very unclear just when and how the end would arrive. Hyung Goo already had all the usual end-stage problems: PCP, CMV, MAC. There was nothing in particular to watch for. There was only the knowledge that most people with all these conditions were already dead.

Hyung Goo and I responded differently to this knowledge. Hyung Goo's attitude was much as it had always been: he saw no reason why he couldn't continue as he was for some time to come. When he was asymptomatic, that had meant years or even decades. Now it meant months, perhaps a year. I responded characteristically as well: I was sure he was going to die, probably soon. As we planned our trip to Boston, I raised the question of whether this might be the last trip. What friends should we try to see? How ought we to handle interactions with family members? Should we try to say goodbye? Should we wait for signals from them about what they did and didn't want to talk about?

Even as we talked, I felt guilty. It seemed I was readier than Hyung Goo was to suppose that we really were near the end. Would he think I had given up on him, that I was itching to have him dead and buried? As the summer wore on, the tension between our perspectives intensified. I was overwhelmed by the stress of working on my dissertation and looking for a job while simultaneously expecting Hyung Goo to die at any moment. And yet, I couldn't just put the dissertation and the job search aside until after he died, because finishing the dissertation and getting a job were things Hyung Goo wanted to live to see me do. It seemed that the only way Hyung Goo could continue to hope for things he wanted to hope for was for me to do things I felt completely incapable of doing.

The dissertation conflict got tangled up with my unhappiness with our living situation. I had long been displacing much of my anger about Hyung Goo's illness onto our apartment, which

161

I loathed. If we just lived in a nicer place, I imagined, then life would be better. One day I went to the laundry room to find sixteen of the eighteen washing machines obviously broken. "That's it!" I announced. "We're moving!" The last thing Hyung Goo wanted to do was move. He raised one objection after another. None of them made any impression on me. Finally he said, "I'm afraid that if you give your time to things like moving, you won't finish the dissertation in time for me to see it." I started to cry. I cried inconsolably for over an hour, to Hyung Goo's puzzlement and alarm. Even I was alarmed at how completely unglued I had become. It seemed that Hyung Goo had inadvertently put his finger on a deeply felt but hardly acknowledged fear: that I would disappoint him.

A couple of days later we were at the clinic. We told Martha the sad story of our emotional upset. Martha's private opinion (she told me later) was that it would be a disaster for us to move, given how sick Hyung Goo was. She couldn't very well say that, so she tried gently to reframe the issue for us: I was looking ahead, wanting to have a life and a house; Hyung Goo's horizons were shrinking as he became more ill, making him just not able to think of things like moving. With respect to my feelings about the dissertation, she was more puzzled. I knew full well that Hyung Goo was horrified at the very idea that I would be afraid of disappointing him. "You should talk to Dan about this," she said. "You seem to have gotten your wires crossed somewhere."

Dutifully, I talked to Dan. But as Martha herself had said, it was too late to expect insight to make me feel better. What was happening to Hyung Goo was just too awful. In the end, both issues were overtaken by events. Hyung Goo was diagnosed with yet another reactivation of his CMV infection, this time in his previously unaffected left eye. As he went back on a twice-a-day induction dose of Ganciclovir, I felt all the wind go out of my sails. I still wanted to move, but I knew I didn't have the energy for it. The dissertation, too, receded into the background as we tended to Hyung Goo's increasingly all-consuming medical routine.

These conflicts notwithstanding, the overall tenor of the summer was one of intense intimacy. We celebrated our fourth wedding anniversary while we were in Boston. We had a two-hour lunch with the minister who had married us. Afterward, we went shopping in the jewelry district. Hyung Goo bought me a pearl pin. In the evening, he gave me a dozen roses and took me out to dinner. It was a lovely day from beginning to end, but with an awful poignancy to it. Would it be our last anniversary?

One evening in midsummer, we watched a movie that ended with the main character weeping over the grave of his wife. We both found this rather unnerving. After we had gone to bed, Hyung Goo said, "I let that stupid movie get to me."

"Yes," I agreed. "It made me think of what it will be like for me to stand over your grave and miss you." In a paroxysm of shared grief unlike any we had experienced before, we both dissolved in tears.

In August, we made our final trip to Tanglewood. On our last evening in Boston, there was a family gathering. Hyung Goo was too tired to take pictures, so I took some. Later I realized I hadn't set the exposure correctly. I was angry with Hyung Goo for not taking the pictures himself. If he had done it, they would have turned out; but I had to do it, and I ruined them, just like I was going to spend the rest of my life having to do things on my own and ruining them. Later that evening I poured out my anger and grief to Hyung Goo, who listened and received me and all my upset feelings with what seemed like bottomless reserves of quiet compassion.

I was back at the hospital early in the morning the day after Hyung Goo was admitted. I was standing next to Hyung Goo's bed, holding his hand, when Martha came in. She went around to the other side of the bed, took Hyung Goo's other hand, and said, "Here we are, Hyung Goo—your two girls!" Over the course of the day, virtually the entire staff of the ID clinic came by Hyung Goo's room and looked in on him. The MICU staff apparently drew the conclusion that any patient with so many

163

staff visitors must be a physician. They addressed him as "Dr. Kim" for the remainder of his stay.

Even in intensive care and on a ventilator, Hyung Goo was busy supervising his medical care. He wanted to know his medications and his dosages and his lab values, and wrote them all down in a little spiral notebook. He wrote his questions for the doctors in the same notebook. The decipherability of his handwriting varied inversely with the depth of his sedation. So did the cogency of his questions, and his ability to understand and remember the answers. I had to be part of all the conversations, trying to understand what the question was, making sure the physicians had answered it, explaining the answer to Hyung Goo, repeating it as often as he asked again.

I was at Hyung Goo's bedside from six in the morning until ten at night every day, going home only to sleep. The MICU actually had strictly limited visiting hours—a couple of hours in the morning, a couple of hours in the afternoon. We proceeded on the assumption that those rules didn't apply to us. One nurse seemed to think they should. I made it clear that while Hyung Goo was her patient, he was my husband, and I was not going to miss entire days of my marriage just because she wanted me to sit in the waiting room. Hyung Goo concurred: "Don't let them kick you out," he wrote. After that there was a note in Hyung Goo's chart saying I was free to care for Hyung Goo as I deemed best.

In his groggy, half-conscious state, Hyung Goo was continually reaching for his tubes. I was just as continually putting his hands down. My seeming interference made him angry. As he pulled his hands away from mine and glared at me, his vagueness evaporated and he was so vividly himself that I burst into tears. Seeing my tears, he forgot both his anger and his tubes, and reached out to comfort me. At other times, the fog of drug-induced dementia settled down around him. He wanted an umbrella, and wouldn't believe my repeated assurance that there was no umbrella. I had to call the resident in to give him the official word. He thought there was a conspiracy by Pepsi-Cola to take over the world. The next day, he wasn't so sure. "No Pepsi conspiracy after all?" he wrote in his notebook, looking sheepish.

John had arrived back in the country around the time that Hyung Goo was admitted to the hospital. He wasn't scheduled to be back in the clinic for a couple of weeks, but he came to the intensive care unit every day to look after Hyung Goo. Hyung Goo was sometimes asleep when John came by, so I conferred with him. I realized during the first of these conversations that I had hardly ever talked with John myself. It was always Hyung Goo and John who talked with each other. They were the team; I was the very interested bystander. Now I had to be on the playing field too.

We waited all day Tuesday for some indication that Hyung Goo was getting either better or worse. We wanted to let his family know he was in intensive care, but we knew their first question would be, "Should we come?"—meaning, "Is he dying right now, or not?" By Wednesday, we still weren't sure. Martha called one of Hyung Goo's brothers, and by evening his father had arrived. His brothers and sister and mother followed over the next couple of days. Our friends Greg and Kate from Princeton were there too. They had been planning to spend the night with us on Tuesday, on their way home from visiting family in Georgia. They came as planned, and stayed. Hyung Goo was very concerned that everyone get the best possible hotel rate, and wrote many notes instructing them to inquire about medical discounts.

By Friday the situation was, if anything, even more nebulous. Hyung Goo's doctors were trying to wean him off the ventilator, gradually reducing the percentage of oxygen and the pressure so his lungs could do more of the work themselves. They weren't meeting with much success. Martha left that day for a week's stay with her parents while her father had elective surgery. We all knew it was probable that Hyung Goo would die while she was gone. She came by his hospital room to say good-bye. "I love you," she said through tears, "and I know you love me, too." Hyung Goo nodded, his eyes burning into hers.

John went out of town that weekend, leaving behind a very nervous MICU staff—they could see how deeply he cared for

Hyung Goo, and they didn't want him dying on their watch. But the weekend went by, and he didn't die. In fact, he seemed to be getting a little better. Hyung Goo's family members started getting restive. They all had responsibilities to get back to. "Anybody have a camera?" Hyung Goo wrote in his notebook. We all knew what he was asking for. Family gatherings always included a group picture. The MICU had rules about how many visitors a patient could have at one time: two. We got the nurse to let us all in at once—Hyung Goo's father and mother, his two brothers and his sister, and me. We gathered around the bed, and the nurse took the picture.

# ABOVE THE CLOUDS

How long will we have? Ever since I had known of Hyung Goo's HIV infection, this had been my question. He had tested HIV-positive five years before we started dating. Lots of people died within five years of infection. It felt like we were living on borrowed time already.

How long will we have? It was impossible to say. We had today, and probably tomorrow, and most likely next week and next month. Next year was always too far away to plan for. Five years was unimaginable. Toward the end of our first year of marriage, several people commented that we were "still newlyweds." We were startled. We didn't think of ourselves as being still near the beginning of our marriage. We thought of ourselves as every day one day closer to the end.

How long will we have? As the horizon drew ever closer, the question took on greater urgency. "Maybe a year, probably less," John said in the spring of 1995. By summer, Hyung Goo had been to death's door and back again. He had countless things wrong with him, and yet seemed relatively stable. It was hard to see that his prognosis had really changed. Maybe a year, probably less.

How long will we have? By August, the uncertainty was overwhelming. How anxious was I supposed to be? If Hyung

167

Goo had another year to live, then maybe I didn't need to panic right away. But maybe he had much less than that. If I wasn't panicked already, would I be caught by surprise?

Then Hyung Goo went into the hospital. Within a week, we knew: he was dying. And with that knowledge, we entered a dimension in which it no longer mattered how long we had. Time itself seemed to have stopped. We still hoped Hyung Goo might be able to get off the ventilator and come home. If he did, he might have some weeks left, maybe even months. But it didn't matter. He was dying, and the question that for so long had seemed so important was suddenly irrelevant. How long would we have? I didn't know, and I didn't care.

We had emerged from the clouds that all our married life had concealed from view the summit of the mountain we had been climbing. The mist was gone; the air was clear and cold and breathtaking. It was still and quiet, the kind of quiet that rings piercingly in your ears, so quiet it was loud. We were at the top. We had reached the summit.

# SEPTEMBER 17, 1995: DEATH

In the photo album from the last year of Hyung Goo's and my life together is the photograph of Hyung Goo in his hospital bed. On one side of the bed are his father and older brother, holding his hand. At his head are his younger brother and his sister, and on the other side of the bed his mother, her hand on his arm, and me, my right hand on the bed rail and both our wedding rings on my left hand. At the center of the picture is Hyung Goo, bare-chested, tubes and wires everywhere, looking straight into the camera through eyes half-closed and clouded with pain and drugs.

I showed the picture to a friend. His response: "Now there's a man in control." I had to look again. It hadn't struck me this way. It had struck me as an excruciating reminder of how awful it had all been. Every one of us in the picture looked like he was having the worst day of his life. And since when was a person in intensive care and on a ventilator "in control"? It was hard to imagine a more dependent posture.

This was not the death that Hyung Goo and I had envisioned for him. We had wanted him to die at home, in a setting that was humane and dignified and private. We agreed to have Hyung Goo put on the ventilator in the hope that it would help him get over his PCP and come home. I felt sure that if he did not get off the vent and come home, I would regret that we had ever come to the hospital at all. I would feel that he had been subjected to the distress of hospitalization and intubation to no good end.

I was wrong. Being on the ventilator was a distressing experience for Hyung Goo, but it gave him the chance he wanted to try and get well one more time. More importantly, as it turned out, his two weeks in intensive care gave him an opportunity to live out the end of his life, and for the two of us to live out the end of our marriage. As it became apparent that he was dying, we had time—time that we would not have had at home—to be with one another, to grieve together at the advent of the separation that we had known would come one day, to remember and cherish our time together, and then to let go and say goodbye.

This was a death that was entirely of a piece with the life that had preceded it. It was a death that included a good deal of suffering, even as his life had included its share of suffering. But it was also a death that was filled with love: for God, for life, for me, his family, and his friends. And it was a death that was characterized by the same kind of intentional presence that Hyung Goo brought to everything and everyone he encountered. "I am HGKim," Hyung Goo wrote in clear block letters on a page of his notebook otherwise filled with indecipherable scrawls. If "control" is a readiness personally to engage all life has to offer, then our friend was right: even in the hospital, in the utter dependence of intensive care and mechanical ventilation, Hyung Goo was very much a man in control.

Over the first ten days of his final hospitalization, Hyung Goo's condition seemed to stabilize and even to improve slightly. He had many visitors, and was busy playing host to them all. "I would like to receive any guests I have," he wrote to the nurse one morning. The conductor of the Duke choirs was with him when another visitor arrived. "Rodney is the best choral conductor in this area," Hyung Goo wrote in his notebook, by way of introduction. My advisor came to see him. "Dr. Wainwright, have you ever thought of writing your memoirs?" Hyung Goo inquired.

"Thanks for coming to visit your almost-dying brother," Hyung Goo wrote to one of his brothers. "Mom, tell about your early childhood," he wrote to his mother. Prompted by his repeated

170

requests to continue, she sat by his bed and talked for hours about her experiences growing up in Japanese-occupied Korea. We had heard some of the stories before, but not nearly all of them. Hyung Goo was afraid he wouldn't remember the details. He had me sit on the other side of the bed and take notes while she talked.

As Hyung Goo's hospital stay stretched into its second week, all the visiting friends and family members began to return home. By the middle of the week, it was just the two of us again. Even as the relatives left, Hyung Goo's condition began to deteriorate. He started spiking fevers. They seemed to indicate a hospital-acquired infection of some kind. His doctors started him on Vancomycin, at that time the antibiotic of last resort. His blood work was looking bad. His organs showed signs of failure. His pneumonia was worse. "Can it be arranged for me to die at home?" Hyung Goo wrote to his doctor. "I would rather be at home, even on a ventilator." Regretfully, John shook his head. Hyung Goo's condition was too unstable for him to be transferred anywhere. If he got better, he could go home; but if he continued to get worse, he would have to die in the hospital.

Dan came to the hospital on Thursday. In most of his previous visits, he had talked only with me. This time, we all seemed to realize he needed to see Hyung Goo. As he entered the room, Hyung Goo found his notebook and began to write. I stood at the head of the bed, puzzling out his wavering script as his pencil formed the letters. He was glad to have known Dan, he wrote, and thankful for the role that Dan had played in my life. "My time is short," he concluded, "maybe only a matter of days; so I want to say, 'Best wishes for the continued success of your personal and family life.'" With Hyung Goo's benediction thus resting on him, Dan took his leave.

The next morning, everything was worse. John came in early to talk with us. We knew what was coming. John and Hyung Goo had had a long-standing agreement with one another that when in John's opinion it was time to let go, he would tell us. We knew that time had come. John sat down by the bed and said, "Hyung Goo, your body is failing. What we can do for you, at this point, is get that tube out, so you can be more comfortable." Hyung Goo was awake and listening, but seemed distant and withdrawn. "Do you understand what I'm saying?" John asked. Hyung Goo nodded. "Do you want some time to think about it?" He nodded again: yes, he did.

When Hyung Goo had been hospitalized the previous spring, it had been brought home to both of us with shocking intensity that we were not ready for him to die. Remembering that, and wanting reassurance for myself, I said to him, "I know you want to live, but do you think you are ready to die?" He shook his head, and it nearly broke my heart. Earlier in the week, he had written a phrase in his notebook: "focusing on God's sovereignty." "Do you remember that?" I asked him. It seemed that we needed to do just that. For reasons we could not understand, it was his time to die, and my time to go on without him, for a while at least. Later in the day, he asked if he had any tests scheduled. I told him again of the blood work that showed the failing of his kidneys and pancreas. "Do you understand what that means?" I asked. He looked at me with an unfathomable sadness in his eyes. He understood.

In the afternoon, Hyung Goo was seized with a desire to put on his shoes and get out of bed—probably, I realized later, an expression of his longing to go home to die. "No," I told him repeatedly. There were too many tubes and wires for him to get out of bed. It was not possible. "WELL TRY" he wrote in angry capital letters. "Does it feel like I'm being mean to you?" I finally asked. Looking tense, baffled, frightened, he nodded: yes, it did. Struggling to speak through tears, I explained: he was on so many drugs that he was just not himself. "But I am taking good care of you, and you can trust me." He nodded again, the tension draining from his body as he leaned back against the pillow.

All that day and evening, we worked on letting go. Hyung Goo was past the point of writing in his notebook. I tried to do the talking for both of us. I talked about all the things he would miss about living—walking in the gardens, seeing his nephews and niece grow up, growing old with me. I talked about our marriage and the happiness we had found together, about what a fine and loving man and husband he was, and how much I loved him and would miss him.

In the afternoon and evening friends came, one by one, to say goodbye. Martha called from her parents' home, very sad, asking me to give Hyung Goo a kiss for her. The last call of the evening was from Dan. He had just gotten off the phone with Trish, John's wife. She had called to say that John was worried that we might not be able to bring ourselves to take the tube out. I reassured Dan. We knew it had to be done; we just hadn't been ready to do it today. We would do it tomorrow.

The night nurses moved Hyung Goo over so I could sleep in his bed with him. I climbed in gingerly, trying to find a place where I wouldn't pull any of his tubes out. As I lay down, he lifted his arm and put it around me, and we settled down together in a manner at least reminiscent of the way we had always done at home. I slept beside him all night there in intensive care, with IV lines trailing across my face and the morphine pump beeping every hour.

The next morning, John came in. "Are you ready to let go?" he asked. Hyung Goo was too far into the process of dying to join with me actively in giving consent. His putting his arm around me the night before had been his last gesture of caring for me. In the morning, he had his job to do, and I had mine. "Yes, we are," I said. John said goodbye to Hyung Goo, and then I said goodbye. I had to leave the room while he was taken off the ventilator. When that was done, I told him, I would come back, and I would stay with him until the end. "Even if you don't know I am here," I said, "I will be with you."

One of our pastors had arrived at the hospital by now. He prayed with Hyung Goo, and then sat in the waiting room with me while Hyung Goo was sedated and extubated. When I got back to his room, he was unconscious and breathing oxygen through a mask. I took my place beside him and waited. It was a longer wait than anyone expected: nearly fourteen hours. It was almost a relief that it took that long. I knew that taking Hyung Goo off the ventilator was a necessary and appropriate act of care for him in his dying, but it had still felt like we were killing him. The fact that it took him fourteen hours to

173

die made his death feel more like something he was doing and less like something we had done to him.

I almost wasn't able to keep my promise not to leave him. In the middle of the day, he spiked a fever. As his metabolism speeded up, he began to thrash about, sitting up and reaching out and opening his eyes. Frantically, I thought, "I'm not going to make it." Even the nurse was distressed, although more for me than for Hyung Goo, who, he felt sure, was not in any way aware of the agitation of his body. Hyung Goo was already getting so much morphine that the nurse hesitated to give him more for fear of killing him outright. Instead, he gave him Tylenol, and waited for that to bring the fever down and thus reduce the rate at which Hyung Goo was metabolizing morphine. As we waited for the fever to abate I began to talk to the nurse about Hyung Goo and about our courtship and marriage, and as I calmed down, Hyung Goo also settled down.

Around midafternoon, I went out to the waiting room and found our minister and his wife. They came back to Hyung Goo's room with me and sat with us for a couple of hours. Eventually they left, and from then on I was mostly alone with Hyung Goo. I lay in bed next to him, holding his hand, listening to him breathe, waiting for him to die.

Late in the evening, Greg and Kate arrived from Princeton. I had called them on Friday, when we knew Hyung Goo was dying, asking them to come. They got in the car on Saturday morning, expecting that Hyung Goo would be gone before they arrived. Kate appeared in the door of Hyung Goo's room, caught sight of the two of us lying down together, and broke into a broad smile with tears just behind it. "That looks so sweet," she said, holding out her arms to me. She and Greg pulled up chairs and sat down by the bed with us.

Just after midnight, Hyung Goo's blood pressure began to drop precipitously. The alarms on the monitors started to go off. The night nurse came in and shut off the alarms, and she and Greg and Kate left the room. Hyung Goo's breath began coming in gasps and shudders, and then there were no more breaths, and he was dead. I knelt beside him in the bed, weeping.

A physician came in and checked Hyung Goo's pupils and his heart, and then paged John. John called Hyung Goo's parents and my parents, all of whom immediately called me. I called our pastor (who had gone home when Greg and Kate arrived) and the funeral director and the minister of Park Street Church and another close friend in Boston. In the middle of the umpteenth telephone call, I realized how distracted I felt. There I was, standing next to Hyung Goo's dead body, talking on the telephone instead of paying attention to him or to me or to whatever needed doing.

I hung up the phone. What did need doing? "I can stand here until I figure it out," I thought. I spent awhile just touching him, feeling the warmth gradually leave his hands and his face, taking in just how dead he really was. Eventually I called Greg and Kate in. We prayed and stood there with him. It felt like all the time in the world wouldn't be enough, and at the same time like there was really nothing left to do.

I decided I didn't want to stay until he was completely cold. We gathered up our things, and Greg and Kate left the room. I stood there a few more minutes with Hyung Goo's body. I touched his forehead. It was like marble—cold, hard, dead. I signed him with the cross, and left. Greg and Kate drove me home. Did I want them to spend the night with me? No, I didn't. I wanted to be in my house by myself, just as I had been every night that Hyung Goo had been hospitalized. They left for their hotel, and I went to bed.

175

# IN MIDAIR

All during Hyung Goo's and my marriage, I found myself incapable of imagining my life without him. How could I possibly live apart from the vocation I had found in being his wife? It would be like free-falling through space, unrelated to anyone or anything, bereft of any sense of purpose or direction.

When Hyung Goo died, I discovered how pale that imagined vision looked alongside the experienced reality. There was in fact a sense of being somewhere in midair, not quite sure which way was up; but the sensation was less like falling off a cliff than it was like being launched from a springboard. I had been flung out of one life and knew only that I had not yet arrived in the next.

# SEPTEMBER 20, 1995:
# FUNERAL

Overnight, everything was different. I had gone into the hospital with Hyung Goo two weeks earlier, a married woman. I emerged without him, a widow. It had been summer still when he entered the hospital. When I came out, it was fall. It seemed that it had been dark the entire time he was hospitalized—it was dark in the mornings when I went to the hospital, and dark in the evenings when I went home to sleep; it had been dark when he was admitted, and dark when he died. I woke up the morning after his death to sunshine.

Perhaps the most striking contrast was between the privacy of dying and the public mourning that followed. Hyung Goo's death had been an intensely private experience. For days I had been in one room with one person doing one thing. When he died, almost instantly, it seemed, I was around countless people, doing countless things, making countless decisions. The disjunction between one day and the next, between horror, intimacy, and solitude on Friday and Saturday, and people, noise, and activity on Sunday, seemed impossible to grasp.

In the next few days and weeks, it seemed as if a set of broad double doors separating Hyung Goo and me from the wider community had been flung open wide. Despite its Dickensian cast of characters, our entire life together had in many ways been very private, the intimacy of romance heightened by the way our circumstances set us apart from virtually everyone else we knew. Now, in the wake of Hyung Goo's death, I found myself transformed from a partner in a marriage that was uniquely ours to the principal mourner among innumerable other mourners. I stood just outside the doorway of the life that had been, blinking owl-like into the light, as family members, colleagues from work and school, medical caregivers, fellow musicians, church members, friends from recent and from distant days gathered around, peering through that opening for one last glimpse of Hyung Goo as we said goodbye to him.

Hyung Goo died at a quarter past midnight. It was 2:30 by the time I got to bed. I was awakened by the telephone. It was our minister calling to ascertain just when Hyung Goo had died, so that the date of his death could be announced in church that morning. Once up, I made a round of phone calls myself, then went to church with Greg and Kate. People gathered around me after the service, offering condolences. I sought out the six other men in our Bible study group. Would they be pallbearers? I spoke with the music director. There were several pieces of music I wanted sung at the funeral. Would she ask the Duke choral director to organize a group to sing them?

In the afternoon, I went to the funeral home and talked with the funeral director about the arrangements. We scheduled the funeral for Wednesday afternoon and the visitation for Tuesday evening. Most of the big decisions had already been made. Hyung Goo was to be cremated, but his body would be present at the visitation and the funeral. The funeral home had a rental casket that we could use, thus sparing us the expense of purchasing a casket only to cremate it. The visitation would be at the funeral home, but the funeral itself would be at Blacknall Church. I was doubly glad for all our planning ahead when confronted with one of the few details yet to be settled: How did I want my name to appear on the thank-you cards? I was completely flummoxed. Mrs. Hyung Goo Kim? Margaret Ault Kim? I had no idea.

Soon after I got back from the funeral home, Martha came over. We sat and talked about Hyung Goo and his death. Martha had never been to our home. Over our sofa were displayed a dozen black-and-white photographs: portraits of our parents and grandparents and other relatives; a photo of Hyung Goo and his brothers when they emigrated from Korea, three solemn little boys in matching shorts and vests. One picture in particular required explanation: a portrait of Hyung Goo in white tie and tails, his head resting on his hand, his gaze dreamy and averted. This picture had been taken by a college classmate on Hyung Goo's twenty-third birthday, just after a Glee Club concert (hence the formal attire). They intended it as a deliberate parody of the self-dramatizing publicity photos favored by so many musicians and other artists. The striking beauty of the photograph, the formality of Hyung Goo's dress, the deeply inward expression on his face, and the fact that the entire thing was a joke all combined to make the portrait a near-perfect crystallization of all that both I and Martha had loved in Hyung Goo.

Dan had offered, earlier in the day, to come by if I needed him. By the time Martha left, I was talked out. I called him and asked if he could come tomorrow. I took a nap, had some dinner, and made a few more phone calls. Greg made many more. All afternoon and into the evening, he was on the telephone calling everyone in our address book to let them know of Hyung Goo's death. Eventually he and Kate left for their hotel. I turned off the ringers on the phones and went up to bed. "A very long day," I wrote in the journal I began that day. "The first day of the rest of my life."

I got up on Monday morning to find three messages on the answering machine already. The home health company sent someone to retrieve Hyung Goo's IV medication and supplies. A friend came over with lunch. She was a medical student, and not squeamish about death. We talked about the whole dying experience as Greg entertained her toddler son.

In the early afternoon, Kate and I went to the funeral home to view Hyung Goo's body. He was dressed in the suit I had brought for him the day before. I was startled to find that his face had been covered with makeup in order to conceal his Kaposi's sarcoma lesions. "Wipe it off," I said. "I'd rather he looked like himself, even with the KS."

179

Dan came by later in the afternoon. We sat and talked for an hour or so. Half an hour after he left, the ministers and music director of the church arrived to discuss the details of the funeral service. For all our efforts at making the practical arrangements, Hyung Goo and I had really done little more than pick the music for the funeral itself. There were several people whom we wanted to make personal remarks; we wanted to have the Lord's Supper celebrated. "That will be fine," they said. "We can take care of the rest."

Greg and Kate and I had dinner at a friend's house. When I got home, I steeled my nerves and put a new message on the answering machine. The old message had been in Hyung Goo's voice. I didn't really want to erase it, or to take upon myself something that had always been "his job," but it seemed a little macabre to leave his voice on the answering machine after he was dead.

Kate spent several hours on Tuesday putting together a display of photographs for the funeral and visitation. I had long wanted there to be such a display, although I had never felt it was something I could discuss with Hyung Goo. It seemed too calculated, like I was really looking forward to the funeral and wanted it to be just right. But in the spring, when it became apparent that we didn't have a lot of time left, I went through the photo albums and picked out thirty or forty of my favorite pictures, located the negatives, and ordered reprints. When Hyung Goo died, the pictures were all sitting in an envelope. Kate went to an art store, bought supplies, and set to work. As she cropped and pasted and decorated and annotated, I sat and watched, soaking up the remembered fullness of our life together.

Relatives arrived throughout the day: Hyung Goo's parents and siblings, my parents and siblings, assorted spouses and children and uncles and aunts. By the end of the afternoon, there were seventeen of us, counting two-month-old Teresa. None of our friends' houses were big enough to accommodate the whole group, so our Bible study group cooked and served us dinner at church: beef tenderloin, rolls, rice, carrots, salad. "Why is the church making us dinner?" someone asked. "Because they want to take care of us," I said.

We went from church to the funeral home for the visitation. Hyung Goo lay in his casket, surrounded by flower arrangements. The casket itself was big and square and upholstered. "It's like being buried in a hotel room," I had complained to the funeral director when we had been discussing the details of the arrangements, years earlier. "Don't they make plain coffin-shaped coffins anymore?" Now the casket didn't seem to matter one way or the other. I had eyes only for Hyung Goo. He looked oddly unlike himself, even with all the makeup wiped off. Only his hands, folded neatly across his body, seemed to look like I remembered them.

More relatives arrived in the course of the visitation. Friends came from church, from school, from work. They greeted me, paused for a moment before the casket, then stood in small groups talking with one another, eventually gravitating to the display of photographs. Voices grew lively; people pointed and laughed. There was Hyung Goo jumping on a trampoline, the shutter catching him just at the top of his bounce so he looked like he was levitating. There we were posing with a cigar-store Indian. We were wearing 3-D glasses; so was the Indian. There was Hyung Goo with a llama at the North Carolina State Fair. With his fingers held up for ears and his face scrunched up like a snout, he looked remarkably like a llama himself. "I never knew Hyung Goo when he wasn't sick," one of the members of our Bible study group said to me. "I had no idea he was so full of life."

I awoke on Wednesday having slept badly, lying awake for hours and with many strange dreams thereafter. I declined invitations from my family and from Hyung Goo's family to get together before the funeral. I just wanted to be by myself and wait. Eventually I got dressed, in a black silk suit I had bought a couple of years earlier, knowing I would wear it to Hyung Goo's funeral. I never showed it to him. Like the photographs, it had seemed too calculated.

Greg and Kate picked me up and we drove together to the funeral home, arriving twenty minutes before everyone else was due, to give me a few minutes alone with Hyung Goo's body. I stood looking at his hands, stroking them. They felt cold, but still familiar, almost comforting. Eventually I joined Greg and Kate in the parlor of the funeral home. It was furnished with uncomfortable Victorian furniture and velvet wall hangings. "It looks like a bordello," Kate said, not unappreciatively.

"Kate, the things you say!" remonstrated Greg.

"My dear, the places I've been!" she replied.

Eventually all the relatives showed up. The funeral home employees ushered us into cars. I had never ridden in a funeral cortège. Now here I was in the front seat of the lead limousine. We followed the hearse to the church. When we got there, the pallbearers were all standing in front of the church, more dressed up than I had ever seen most of them, with white carnations in their lapels. "This is a lot easier than planning a wedding," I thought. "I didn't have to do a thing about those boutonnières."

The pallbearers took the casket out of the hearse and carried it up the long flight of stairs to the second-floor sanctuary. The two ministers and I followed the casket into the church, accompanied by Greg and Kate and all the other relatives. The funeral director ushered us into the front pews, and we sat down. "You looked so small," someone said to me later, "and your eyes were open wide."

A quartet of friends from Duke and from church rose and sang the *Kyrie* from the William Byrd *Mass for Four Voices*. This was music written for Catholics practicing their religion in secret in the time of Queen Elizabeth I. It sounded like music for a time of suffering and sorrow: plaintive, yet sustaining. *"Kyrie elison. Christe eleison. Kyrie eleison."* "Lord have mercy. Christ have mercy. Lord have mercy."

We all joined in the opening hymn. "I greet thee, who my sure Redeemer art, my only trust and Savior of my heart, who pain didst undergo for my poor sake; I pray thee from our hearts all cares to take . . ." Would I be able to sing? For the previous several Sundays, every time I had tried I had begun to cry. But I wanted to sing this hymn. I didn't want to have to retreat from it, or from anything else in the service. I wanted to be completely focused and participating in everything. This was the only funeral Hyung Goo would ever have, and I wanted to be there for it.

It almost seemed as if Hyung Goo himself were there for it. The senior pastor stood and read the Old Testament lection and the psalm. As his resonant bass voice filled the sanctuary, it was as if through him the psalmist were giving voice to all the sorrow and hope Hyung Goo had ever known. "I waited patiently for the LORD; he inclined to me and heard my cry. He drew me up from the desolate pit, out of the miry bog, and set my feet upon a rock, making my steps secure. He put a new song in my mouth, a song of praise to our God. . . ."

The associate pastor rose and read the epistle and the gospel lections. "Lo! I tell you a mystery. We shall not all sleep, but we shall all be changed, in a moment, in the twinkling of an eye, at the last trumpet. For the trumpet will sound, and the dead will be raised imperishable, and we shall be changed . . ." "Peace I leave with you; my peace I give to you; not as the world gives do I give to you. Let not your hearts be troubled, neither let them be afraid." He preached the sermon. Suffering is real, he said, and so is redemption. We said the creed. ". . . I believe in the holy catholic church, the communion of saints, the resurrection of the body and the life everlasting, Amen."

Greg went forward to deliver the first of the eulogies. He would focus, he said, on Hyung Goo's three great loves: his music, his God, and his wife—"to put them in roughly chronological order." The congregation, tense with grief, relaxed in laughter, then hung on Greg's every word as he led us through Hyung Goo's life: his conducting and singing, his journey away from Christian faith and back to it, our relationship in its beginnings and growth. It had been touching, Greg said, to be present with Hyung Goo during his last days and see the support offered him by his church and his family. "I think Hyung Goo left this life knowing he was deeply loved by his family, his friends, his wife, and his God."

183

Martha spoke next. She described the ways in which she had worked with Hyung Goo and with both of us in so many of the issues that all people with AIDS confront, including those related to confidentiality: Whom do I tell? When do I tell them? How do I tell them? Because Hyung Goo was so open about his illness, she observed, many people did and would continue to view people with AIDS differently for having known him, and she herself had been deeply affected through her relationship with him. "I began as Hyung Goo's social worker," she said. "Today I say goodbye to Hyung Goo, my friend."

The leader of our Bible study group was last. Hyung Goo had come into the group with great needs, Steve noted, and yet he had served others by his interest in them and by his compassion for them. Even the children in the group had sensed that interest and compassion: Steve's five-year-old son, on being told of Hyung Goo's death, responded, "But he was my friend!" "We never knew Hyung Goo in health," said Steve, "and yet in his weakness and his suffering he gave much to all of us." I sat listening to each of the speakers in turn with two thoughts uppermost in my mind: "I am so privileged to have been this man's wife," and "This is a great funeral!"

A friend stood and sang the Handel aria whose first words Hyung Goo had had inscribed on his gravestone: "I know that my Redeemer liveth, and that he shall stand at the latter day upon the earth . . ." The minister prayed, and the quartet sang the Mozart *Ave Verum Corpus.* "Hail, true body, born of the Virgin Mary. Thou who truly suffered, sacrificed upon the cross for humankind, whose side was pierced, whence the stream of blood did flow: be to us a foretaste of the trial of death." And with that, we celebrated the Lord's Supper. "If you want to know what hope tastes like," said the minister, "this is it."

The congregation rose to sing the final hymn. "For all the saints, who from their labors rest, who thee by faith before the world confessed, thy name, O Jesus, be forever blessed; Alleluia! Alleluia!" On and on the singing went, verse after verse after verse. "From earth's wide bounds, from ocean's farthest coast, through gates of pearl streams in the countless host, singing to Father, Son, and Holy Ghost; Alleluia! Alleluia!" As

184

the final notes echoed around us, the minister pronounced the commendation and the benediction, and it was done. We had said goodbye.

The pallbearers, with the casket, left the sanctuary first, followed by me and all the family members. I emerged from the church into crisp air and blue sky and brilliant sunshine, and watched the pallbearers carry the casket down the steps of the church and put it in the hearse. We had just confessed our faith in the communion of saints. Now here it was in front of me. These were the people who had been carrying us along through all of Hyung Goo's illness. When they could do nothing more for us than carry his body, they carried his body. Each pallbearer took the white carnation from his lapel and laid it on the casket. They shut the door of the hearse, and I walked past it and around to the side door of the church and back in for the reception.

The first person to greet me was Martha, followed by all the relatives, and then everyone else. It seemed that everyone was crying but me. It also seemed that everyone wanted to hug me. I was happy to receive the first few hugs, but I was unsure that I wanted to hug all hundred and fifty or so people who had attended the funeral. Dan, for example, was standing in the line of people waiting to greet me. Would he hug me? Yikes! Happily, the mode of greeting had subsided to a handshake by the time Dan got to me. Geoffrey Wainwright was not far behind him. "I'm glad to see there are still churches that can put on a good funeral!" he said.

So was I.

185

# AT THE WHEEL

I had felt so out of control for so long. The inexorable progression of Hyung Goo's illness, the interminable slog of graduate study, the unrelenting psychological turmoil both revealed and created by psychotherapy, our apartment complex with its eternally broken washing machines—I felt equally defeated by all of it. My life and self seemed like a boat that I was sure was going to capsize at any moment. I couldn't tell whether I felt more seasick or terrified. All I wanted to do was huddle in the gunwales and throw up over the side.

Did it have to be like this? Most people didn't seem to be nearly as undone by their lives as I was by mine, but the reason seemed to be that they just weren't paying attention. Was that the choice—sleepwalk through life and feel relatively okay, or pay attention and feel awful?

One day late in the spring of 1995, feeling even more overwhelmed than usual, I sought out a friend to talk to. In the course of the conversation, I realized that here was a person who lived life intensely and yet was not undone by it. He saw challenges as bracing rather than overwhelming; he was able to trust and not bound by fear; he was eager to see clearly and to know the truth, whether that truth were painful and ugly or good and beautiful. If Allan's life were a boat, I thought, he

186

would be standing in the bow, braced against the spray, exhilarated by the adventure of it all.

I told another friend about this conversation, and the difference between Allan's boat and mine. He laughed. "Someday," he said, "you'll be at the steering wheel of your boat."

Within a day of Hyung Goo's death, I knew: I was there. It was as if his death and all the events associated with it had catapulted me into the pilot house. The sea was choppy; the weather was changeable; but I had my hand on the wheel. Hyung Goo had trusted me with his life, and I had not disappointed him. He died knowing he was loved beyond all measure, knowing he was worthy of that love, knowing I was with him to the end. If I could do that, I could do anything.

# OCTOBER 7, 1995: BURIAL

Hyung Goo hadn't gotten to go home to die. He did go home to be buried. "Home," in this case, meant Boston. We had met in Boston and married in Boston. Our friends were there; the chorus was there. Our families both had roots there. By some strange stroke of providence, we both had grandparents buried in the same cemetery in west suburban Boston. My father's parents had lived in Newton for sixty years, and were buried there when they died. Hyung Goo's maternal grandfather had lived his entire life in Korea, but had been brought to Boston by his children for medical care at the end of his life. When he died, he too was buried in the Newton cemetery. It seemed the natural place for Hyung Goo to be buried as well.

In the summer of 1994 we went to the cemetery to choose a gravesite. We had decided that Hyung Goo would be cremated, since this would make it easier (and cheaper) to transport his remains to Boston from wherever he died. It also multiplied the burial options. We could purchase an "urn garden" plot, in which only cremated remains could be buried. Or we could choose a single grave (which could hold two caskets, stacked one on top of the other, or two cremated remains), or a double grave (which could hold four caskets or four urns). And did we want a headstone or a flat marker? Headstones were permitted only on double graves; single graves and urn garden plots were limited to markers laid flush to the ground. What about location? An older part of the cemetery? A newer part? Near a pond? Near trees? And what about the marker? Granite?

188

Marble? Bronze? What did we want it to say? Did we want both our names on it, or only Hyung Goo's?

Practically hyperventilating from the multiplicity of choices and the emotionally charged nature of the subject, I described the options to Dan in a telephone conversation. "You don't have to make this decision right away, do you?" he asked. In fact, we did, or had made up our minds that we did. Who knew when Hyung Goo would die? The last thing I wanted to do between his death and his burial was fly to Boston to purchase a gravesite. I wanted it chosen and paid for and ready to go.

Eventually we decided on an urn garden plot beside a little bridge over a pond. There were flowers next to the bridge, and flowering trees nearby: a magnolia, a redbud, a weeping cherry. It reminded me of the Duke gardens, where Hyung Goo and I spent so much time. "I like the idea of that weeping cherry blooming over his grave, year after year," I wrote to Dan. "Well, I don't know that I *like* it, exactly, but it seems to supply a link between where he will be buried and where we have actually lived our married life."

Across the street from the cemetery was a memorial company. There were rules, they told us, about what one could or could not put on a marker in any given section of the cemetery. Among things not permitted in our section was the depiction of human body parts. "Great heavenly days!" I thought. "What do they think people would put on their gravestones if they didn't have that rule?" It turned out that the prohibition was aimed at things like praying hands or the sacred heart of Jesus. As we walked around the sample displays we saw plenty of other things the rule would exclude, among them sentimentalized crucifixes and pictures of Jesus and Mary that, had they been in color, would certainly have had blue eyes and blond hair. It didn't break my heart to know that none of these emblems of bad taste would ever show up on a grave near Hyung Goo's.

If we were willing to think ahead, the memorial company people told us, we could have the stone placed on the grave before the interment. That way, friends or family who traveled some distance to come to the burial and who would not be back for some time, if ever, could see the stone and know what the grave would look like. The greater sense of finality that this might provide for people at the burial service appealed to us. It took us another year to made our final decisions about the grave marker. The stone was cut and installed in August of 1995, in time for us to see it before our last trip to Tanglewood.

I was awakened the day after Hyung Goo's funeral by the telephone. It was the funeral director, calling to say someone would be coming by with the flower arrangements from the service. There were a lot of them. "All these flowers make the house look like a funeral parlor itself," I remarked to the deliveryman. "I should pile them up in the living room and then lie down on the couch."

"Heh, heh," he said, weakly, and fled.

We had planned for a two- or three-week delay between Hyung Goo's funeral and his burial and accompanying memorial service, in order to give friends and family from out of town an opportunity to make travel plans if they wanted to attend. I sent printed notices of Hyung Goo's death and of the scheduled services to everyone we knew. I asked a friend from the chorus to organize a group to sing at the memorial service. A friend who was a pianist would accompany a movement from the Brahms *German Requiem*, as well as the same Handel aria as had been sung at the funeral.

I mailed a thick packet with the other music for the service to the organist: accompaniments to the hymns, the Mozart *Ave Verum Corpus*, the opening portion of a funeral composition by the Baroque composer Heinrich Schütz, a particular Bach fantasia to be played as the postlude. The organist at Park Street Church was new since Hyung Goo and I had been married there. Years later, I encountered him at a social function. Neither of us could quite place the other. In an effort to jog both our memories, I explained my connection to Park Street: "My late husband and I were married there, and he was buried from there. I can't remember who played the organ for his memorial service . . ."

190

"I did," said the organist, a look of dawning recognition on his face. "You sent me quite a bit of music."

The burial and memorial service were scheduled for a Saturday. I flew to Boston the preceding Thursday. On Friday morning I went to the cemetery office to see the urn containing Hyung Goo's remains. Hyung Goo and I had not gotten around to choosing an urn before he died, and I had had to select one at my visit to the funeral home immediately following Hyung Goo's death. I had opted for an inoffensively plain buff-colored marble vase near the bottom of the price range, eschewing some very expensive cast bronze monstrosities covered with dolphins. I had not seen the urn since, as the funeral home had arranged to have it shipped directly to the cemetery following the cremation.

The cemetery clerk brought out the urn, placed it on a table, and left me alone with it. What was I supposed to do, now that I was face to face with it? I was sorry I had had the urn shipped directly to the cemetery, and wished I had thought instead to take it home with me for a few days first. Then I could just have lived with it for a little while, instead of trying to think of what to do. It was too late for that now, so I looked at it, and touched it, and just sat there with it. Hyung Goo's parents had asked if they could have the urn at their house overnight before the burial. That sounded fine to me, and like something Hyung Goo would have welcomed. I signed the appropriate consent forms, and they came and got the urn and took it home with them.

I was staying with friends nearby. It rained all morning the day of the burial, but by midday was barely misting. We drove to the cemetery. The few relatives there when we arrived grew to over seventy as the scheduled time approached. Hyung Goo's parents and siblings arrived. His older brother was carrying the urn, wrapped in a piece of Korean silk. We piled into cars to drive to the gravesite, the cemetery workmen leading us in procession through the cemetery. The leaves were changing, and the trees glowed with color against the overcast sky.

The minister who had married Hyung Goo and me was conducting the service. He gathered the crowd around the open

191

grave, Hyung Goo's brother lowered the urn into the ground, and the service began. It was short, as I had known it would be: Scripture readings, liturgical readings, and prayer, followed by the Lord's Prayer. Halfway through, I could feel the tears brimming over. I didn't want to fumble in my handbag for a tissue for fear I'd miss something. Fortunately, by the time my nose started to drip, it was almost over, and I could go for the tissue.

When the minister had finished, Hyung Goo's father spoke for a few minutes, first in Korean and then in English, inviting people to the memorial service that would follow at Park Street Church. The relatives began to mill about and greet me and one another. I stood waiting for one of the cemetery workmen to come and fill in the grave. I wasn't about to go off and leave Hyung Goo sitting there in an open grave. Eventually I had to go find the workman and tell him I wanted the grave closed before I left. I watched as he shoveled in the dirt and tamped it down and filled in with more dirt. There were a couple of bouquets of flowers on the grave. I picked a white rose from one of them and took it with me.

We drove in to Park Street. The church was bustling with people preparing the reception and arriving for the service. I went upstairs to the sanctuary to speak with the musicians: twenty singers, plus the pianist and the organist. As I turned to go back downstairs, I nearly collided with a stranger in a Salvation Army uniform. I knew instantly who he was—a college roommate of Hyung Goo's who, after several years as a high-priced lawyer, had decided he would rather be in the Salvation Army. He was stationed in Los Angeles, and had flown across the country to be at the service.

Greg and Kate had driven up from Princeton to attend the burial. Greg would repeat his eulogy at the memorial service. I waited downstairs with them and the ministers as the time for the service approached. At a few minutes past the appointed hour, we went upstairs and took our places. The singers went forward to sing the Schütz, and the service began. "*Nacket bin ich von Mutterleibe kommen; nacket werde ich wiederum dahinfahren.*" "Naked came I out of my mother's womb; naked

192

shall I return thither. The Lord gave and the Lord hath taken away; blessed be the name of the Lord."

Suddenly I was exhausted. It had been three weeks since Hyung Goo's death. It was time to be done with funerals and burying and memorial services. Readings, prayers, kind words from friends—I was ready for it all to be over. As the singers stood and relaxed into the Brahms—a piece they knew so well they could have sung it in their sleep—I felt as if I myself were asleep, or nearly so, floating atop the music as a feverish child floats on a mother's lullaby. "How lovely is thy dwelling place, O Lord of hosts! . . . Blessed are those who dwell in thy house, ever singing thy praise!"

Communion went on forever. There seemed to be hundreds of people there, all coming forward to receive. It was as if the history of both our lives were being replayed before me: friends of mine and of Hyung Goo's from college, graduate school, work, church, musical groups; friends of our families; relatives from as far away as California and England; people I knew and people I didn't know. Finally it was finished. The congregation sang *For All the Saints*. I started to cry midway through the fourth verse from equal parts of grief and exhaustion. The minister gave the benediction, and I headed down the back stairs to the reception as the organist began the postlude. The words of the chorale were printed in the bulletin. "Christ Jesus lay in death's strong bands, for our offenses given. But now at God's right hand he stands, and gives us bread from heaven. Wherefore let us joyful be, and sing to God right thankfully, Loud songs of Alleluia! Alleluia!"

And with that, I was done. Hyung Goo's burial and memorial service had been the last scheduled events. I had checked off the last items on my list of things to do before I died.

# WASTELAND

When Hyung Goo died, I stopped crying. I had been crying more or less nonstop in the hospital for two weeks. My nose was raw from those awful hospital tissues and from the paper towels I would use when I couldn't find the tissues. But when Hyung Goo died, the tears dried up. It reminded me of the story in the book of Samuel where King David's son is dying. David cries and cries; but when the child dies, he stops crying. It felt like that—Hyung Goo died, and the tears were gone. It wasn't a decision; it was an event, an experience. An experience of barrenness, of being empty even of tears.

The crying started up again shortly. The barrenness lasted a long time. It was like being on a mountaintop above the tree line, with low clouds overhead, able to see only sideways, neither up into the sky nor down into the valley, with only bare ground and rocks and windswept snow all around. It seemed that all ways were the same. There was nowhere to go: no direction, no time, no path, no destination.

I could feel the tug toward opting out of any more mountain climbing. It had taken so long to get up here. It was so cold. I could just lie down in the snow and go to sleep. It wouldn't be a very honorable thing to do, to refuse to grieve, to choose death over life. What was the alternative? Which way was down? I couldn't tell. I was in the midst of a vast wasteland; it seemed to go on and on forever, utter bleakness stretching out before me farther than the eye could see.

194

# RECONNAISSANCE

Hyung Goo and I began our marriage with the knowledge that there were things we longed for but would never have: a houseful of children, a home of our own to put them in, many years to share with one another. By the end of our marriage, we had lost most of what we started out with: the strength to work, to sing, to study and read and travel and participate in the wider world of people and places and activity. We went directly from being young to being old. Our life was lived in the triangle of home and hospital and church, each within a half mile of the others. Hyung Goo watched the weather on the television several times a day, as one of the only ways left to him of being connected with the outside world.

A few days before Hyung Goo's death, a friend came to the hospital to sing for him. ". . . Yea, though I walk in death's dark vale, yet will I fear no ill, For thou art with me, and thy rod and staff me comfort still. My table thou hast furnished in presence of my foes; My head thou dost with oil anoint, and my cup overflows . . ." As I listened to the familiar words, it dawned on me: these things had all been true for us. All our married life, I had been furious that we had had to live with the shadow of death looming over us. And yet, we had had a table prepared before us; even death standing there looking at us couldn't take away all that we had received and enjoyed together. It seemed as if the goods of marriage were present more intensely in that hospital room than they had ever been before: we were more truly husband and wife, trusting one another, caring for one

195

another, in the midst of all that suffering and horror, than at any other time.

It seemed as if the entire universe had contracted into that hospital room. Our life, that looked so tiny from the outside, was enormous on the inside. There were worlds within worlds, each one bigger than the one before. It was like living in the midst of the mystery of the incarnation, in which a stable held the creator of the universe. Who could have imagined there could be so much to know in another person? Who could have imagined there could be so many places to go in relationship with one another? "The two of you did more together, at the end, than any other couple I have ever known," Martha told me later. We had been going farther and farther toward the center, into the bigger and bigger worlds that lay within. In the wake of Hyung Goo's death, my job was to make the journey in reverse. It was time to begin to spiral out again into worlds farther from that center, from which I could look back and wonder at what had been.

Months after Hyung Goo's death, I was still astonished at the grace with which he had died. It seemed to me that he had died obediently, neither desiring death nor fearing it, loving life but recognizing that it was his time to die. Only a couple of years earlier he had been so frightened. He had been facing the decision to leave work, which at the time seemed tantamount to dying. But by the time he died, he wasn't frightened any more, not as he had been before. If he felt fear, it was the fear that distinguishes the brave man from the fool, the fear that any wise person feels in the face of the unknown. It seemed there had been more fear in the anticipation of what might happen than there was in the actual experience.

While his fear had diminished, his suffering had only increased. Hyung Goo hadn't called attention to that suffering, and I hadn't really wanted to think about it. We were both trying so hard to focus on living and loving one another and doing things together that we enjoyed. But he did in fact suffer a great deal—pain, nausea, sleeplessness, endless medical routines, loss of physical powers, loneliness, and just plain feeling unwell most of the time. And yet it seemed that his temperament only got sweeter. He only loved me more; he only was more patient, only wanted more to understand me and to comfort me and to be with me. The transformation was breathtaking, from one so wounded to one so whole, so vibrant and joyful and secure.

In Hyung Goo I saw the weak made strong and the poor made rich. I saw it in his life, and I saw it in his death, luminously and unmistakably. Here were all the reversals so central to the gospel: life in the midst of death, healing in the midst of illness, thankfulness in the midst of loss, strength made perfect in weakness. This was what redemption looked like, and it was incomprehensible.

I felt like Job must have felt when he said, "I had heard of thee by the hearing of the ear, but now my eye sees thee. I despise myself, and repent in dust and ashes." Job had been complaining vigorously about his suffering for a long time: "Who do you think you are, to allow these things to happen to me? I know what's good for me; give it to me, now!" Finally God answered him: "Where were you when I laid the foundations of the earth?" In other words, "I'm God and you're not." And Job's response was, "Oh."

That's how I felt. I was working on a Ph.D. in theology. I knew all the answers. I knew that God is good, that God is in charge, that God's wisdom is sometimes inscrutable, but that doesn't make him any less good or any less in charge. And I had been railing against God for years, sure that God was out to get me and out to get Hyung Goo, that Hyung Goo's illness and anticipated death were an unmitigated disaster, a sign of, if not God's abandonment, then God's total lack of appropriate concern and care for us.

In Hyung Goo's death, I saw what it seemed that before I had only heard: that love is stronger than death, that redemption is not compensation but transformation. And I was dumbstruck, speechless, like I had had the wind knocked completely out of me. I realized that I was not in charge, and it was a good thing, too. The one who was in charge was up to things utterly beyond my comprehension, and it was not my job to judge; it was my job to be awestruck. I had no more answers to my

197

questions than I had had before—Why me? Why him?—but I had nothing more to say. All I could do was cry.

The last five or six months of Hyung Goo's life began to appear in a new light. Our church's service of prayers for Hyung Goo's healing had taken place in February. Six weeks later Hyung Goo entered the hospital to start Foscarnet, and nearly died of kidney failure. I had thought, "If this isn't exactly the opposite of an answer to prayer, I don't know what would be." In June, a friend said to me, "I am sure that in the providence of God you will have Hyung Goo for as long as you need him." I wanted to slug him. I thought, "I wish I were needier, so I'd have him for longer."

Hyung Goo died in September. He had spent the spring writing a memoir. Every evening we talked about what he had written that day, remembering together his life and our life. In June we traveled to his class reunion and saw our friends and families in Boston and New York. In August we met his three-week-old niece and made our final trip to Tanglewood. None of these things made Hyung Goo feel that he was finished with the business of living, but they gave both of us the sense that we had done some things that really needed to be done while there was still time. It was so much better to have done them than not to have done them, even if death still came far too soon.

In those last five or six months we moved from being unprepared for Hyung Goo to die, to being ready. It was as if all our married life we had been laying a foundation that would be strong enough to support us as together we met Hyung Goo's death. In April, the foundation was still incomplete. By September, it was finished.

I found myself looking back to that hospitalization in April, when Hyung Goo could so easily have died, and wondering whether maybe those last five months were God's answer to our prayer. It wasn't the answer I wanted. I wanted Hyung Goo to get well; I wanted him to wake up in the morning miraculously better. But what we got was five more months together, five months in which we learned and grew and loved and hoped and grieved and remembered and said goodbye. We could so easily not have had any of it. Those months came as such a gift; they were precious beyond words.

Even to think in such terms was profoundly unnerving. To call Hyung Goo's last months an answer to prayer seemed too close to denying how awful it was that he had died, how heart-broken we were that he wasn't healed, that we didn't get what we wanted, even though we asked, even though we pleaded. But both were true—we didn't get what we wanted above all else, and we got something of incomparable value. We got time to live out the end of our marriage. Our friend was right: I did have Hyung Goo for as long as I needed him.

As those last months and weeks began to come into focus, so did the many individual gifts and givers that had filled them. We had been cared for so generously by so many people. Dan, who had no professional connection with Duke Medical Center, had been at the hospital every other day during Hyung Goo's final illness. "I hope you realize how unusual this is," a friend who was a psychologist said to me. "In my ten years as a therapist, I've never visited anyone in the hospital." This wasn't strictly true—my psychologist friend worked with the criminally insane. They were always in the hospital. But I took his point. Dan had extended himself to us in ways that went far beyond the requirements of professionalism.

So had Martha. Her response to Hyung Goo's death was colored with enormous relief. She had known, in a way we could not have, just how bad it could have been. She was so thankful that Hyung Goo had not lived long enough to lose all his vision, that he had not become so thin and wasted as to be disfigured, that he had not suffered from any perceptible degree of dementia, as the vast majority of AIDS patients eventually did. On the contrary, he retained his mental clarity right to the end—although, as she observed, this had made saying goodbye to him that much more wrenching. He was so present, right to the very end.

John had borne the burden of that mental clarity most intensely, as he led not only me but Hyung Goo himself through the decision to discontinue use of the ventilator. John had known the tube needed to come out the moment he knew that Hyung Goo was dying. And yet, he neither forced that knowledge on us nor abandoned us to our own ignorance, neither making the decision for us nor offering to do whatever we wanted. Rather, he both guided us and waited for us. John had cared for dying patients many times before, but we were meeting death for the first time. To make the decision that needed to be made, we needed both his patience and his help. We knew we could trust him for both.

"Anyone can treat condition 'x'," John said to me later. "The real difference is in the last few months or weeks of life." We saw that difference in John's care for us. It was a difference that cost him dearly. His wife's late-night telephone call to Dan, conveying John's fear that we would not be able to bring ourselves to consent to removal of the ventilator, only began to suggest just how achingly sad it had been to accompany yet another patient to his death. After Hyung Goo's funeral and memorial service, I wrapped up the display of photographs that Kate had prepared and took it in to the clinic. Martha set it up so the staff could see it. A month or so later, I saw John at an AIDS benefit concert. He thanked me for having brought the photographs in. "I've paused before them on many occasions, just taking them in," he said. "It's made it easier."

Greg and Kate were perhaps the most undone of all our care-givers. Neither they nor we had had any idea that they would play so prominent a part in Hyung Goo's final illness and death. What had been planned as a simple overnight visit turned into weeks spent accompanying Hyung Goo and me through his death, and then me alone through his funeral and memorial service. Later that fall a friend who was a gerontologist mentioned that she had had a long conversation with Greg about the prospect of removing Hyung Goo from the ventilator. She dealt with end-of-life issues all the time, but Greg had never done so. Together they had discussed a range of his questions and concerns.

For the first time it dawned on me how much of the story of Hyung Goo's illness and death I would never know. That story was not all about me, or even all about us. Every one of the people whose lives had intersected with ours had his or her own experience of Hyung Goo and his life and death. In Greg and Kate's case, that experience had been deeply complex, even traumatic, as with virtually no preparation they had simultaneously cared for us and coped with their own grief. Kate told me later that she and Greg spent months just pulling themselves back together in the wake of those several weeks.

All fall I wrote thank-you notes. A letter to the staff of the Medical Intensive Care Unit. A letter to the staff of the Infectious Diseases Clinic. Letters to our pastors at Blacknall and Park Street, to the musicians who had performed at the services, to the friends who had sent flowers, who had been eulogists, who had made memorial gifts to the clinic or to the Duke gardens, who had written to tell me of their memories of Hyung Goo and their sorrow at his death.

Night after night I sat at the dining-room table, writing to one or another of scores of people scattered all over the world. They came from so many different places. Their connections to us were so various. And now ties of gratitude bound me to each of them in such complex and far-reaching ways. What in each instance was I thankful for? What need had this person seen and met? What words should I choose to thank him or her?

In the book of Samuel there is a story in which God gives the people of Israel victory over their enemies, and in thanksgiving they set up a stone and call it Ebenezer, Stone of Help, saying, "Thus far has the Lord helped us." It felt as if that was what I was doing in saying thank you to all these people. I was heaping up little piles of rocks, marking the places where these friends had given of themselves to me. Our lives were linked by my loss and their gift. My gratitude, and its expression, served to mark the place where that link was forged.

Those little piles of rocks became the markers in my wilderness. Even as actual piles of stones are used to mark trails that lie above the tree line, so these metaphorical piles of stones marked a path through the austere barrenness of grief. The path was not in front of me, but behind me. It was made of countless gifts of caring, and I was marking it as I paused and reflected and thanked the givers of those gifts.

I didn't feel better for saying thank you. I felt reminded, vividly and concretely, that I had been helped thus far. In the midst of the vast emptiness of Hyung Goo's death, there was a presence: the presence of the friends and neighbors, pastors and doctors who had cared for us, and who continued to care for me. If there was a path forward to be found, I would find it only in their company.

# FLOOD STAGE

Six weeks after Hyung Goo's death, I went to the eye doctor for a routine appointment. I was overwhelmed by all the questions posed in the course of the exam: "Clearer here? Or here?" I didn't know. I couldn't tell. At the end of the exam, I couldn't get my eyes to focus together. "I'm sorry," I said to the eye doctor. "This just takes more energy than I've got."

"How come you've got so little energy?" he inquired.

"My husband died," I said.

"What?" he said.

"My husband died," I repeated dully. "A few weeks ago."

"What happened?" the doctor asked.

"He had AIDS . . . He'd been sick for a long time," I said, and started to cry. The doctor handed me a tissue and offered his condolences. I sat in the examination chair and wept.

A few months later, I was at church. Toward the end of the service, during communion, I started to cry. I sat there and sobbed for some time. The young man sitting next to me, whose face was familiar but whose name I couldn't quite remember, said, "It's hard to see you hurting so and not be able to do anything. It makes me cry."

"Well, at least I have company," I said.

203

"You seem a very independent person," he said. I didn't know what to say, and remained silent. "Maybe that is true in some senses and not in others," he ventured.

"I liked having Hyung Goo here to take care of me," I said.

"Really?" he said.

"Really," I said, and started to cry again. He put his arm around me, and I put my head on his shoulder and sobbed, at the same time thinking, "I don't even know this man!"

Scenes like this were the story of my life for at least a year after Hyung Goo died. I never left the house without wads of Kleenex in my pockets. I was always bursting into tears, usually in utterly unsuitable circumstances, and I just didn't care.

I felt as flooded by my experiences as by my tears. When rain falls on earth already saturated with water, there is nowhere for that rain to go, and a flash flood ensues. It was like that for me with emotion. Every circumstance I encountered was fraught with feeling, but I was already so waterlogged that I had nowhere to put any of it.

So I wrote it all down. The day that Hyung Goo died a friend said to me, "This is a sacred time. You need to pay attention; you need to remember. You should keep a journal." I began that night. Every day I wrote down everything that had happened, every conversation I had had, every thought that had passed through my head, just so the runoff had somewhere to go.

# ALMOST NOBLE

It had felt so worthwhile to love Hyung Goo, and so incomparably satisfying to be loved by him. With his death, I felt limp, deflated, utterly without purpose. Of course there were things to be done: settle the estate, finish my degree, get a job. But none of them mattered. If I died in the middle of them, it wouldn't really make any difference. It seemed I had decades and decades ahead of me, and nothing of any consequence to do in them. I had already finished my life's work.

The sense of aimlessness only increased with the new year. I was leaving behind a year most of which Hyung Goo and I had shared, a year that had been characterized by a constant sense of urgency as we raced to live as fully as we could as fast as we could, before the curtain rang down. I was beginning a year we would never share, a year in which nothing was urgent, a year in which I felt unable to do anything because I didn't know what to do or where to start.

One evening I found myself at church, listening to a sermon on forgiveness and gratitude and humility. The pastor's words evoked vividly the loss of Hyung Goo's forgiving, thankful, humble presence. Somewhere in the middle I started to cry. By the end of the service I was completely undone. A friend who was sitting next to me put his arms around me, and I sat there with my face in my hands and sobbed.

This friend was no stranger to loss. He was an orphan; his parents had been murdered twenty-two years earlier, when he was twelve. He had hardly begun to feel his grief for them until years after their deaths. "To see you in the midst of such grief for Hyung Goo feels good and right to me," he said to me after the service. "I see you doing what I wish I had done at the time for my parents. It is an awful, awful loss; it feels terrible. The only right thing to do is to cry and cry and cry. In a society so oriented toward pleasure, really to feel pain and express it is almost noble."

I did have a job to do in the weeks and months and years following Hyung Goo's death. My job was to grieve. I was teaching an undergraduate class in theological ethics the semester that Hyung Goo died. Other graduate students and faculty members filled in for me during his hospitalization and for several weeks after his death. I returned to teaching after fall break, and managed somehow to get to the end of the semester. I turned down opportunities to teach in the spring. Much later, on learning that I had taught one course in the fall and none in the spring of that year, someone said to me, "What did you *do*?"

"I grieved," I said. It was like caring for a tiny infant. Every new mother has stumbled through that sleep-deprived haze in which it seems the baby is perpetually either currently squalling, recently squalling, or soon-to-be squalling, surrounded by piles of laundry that isn't going to get done and dishes that aren't going to get washed, because as soon as the baby has been dressed and fed and burped and changed and rocked and soothed it is time to do it all over again, and there is not a particle of either time or energy left over for anything else.

Grief was like that, only sadder. Most mothers are falling in love with their babies at the same time as they are exhausted by them. I was far more absorbed in letting go of an old life than in greeting a new life. I felt so completely defined by Hyung Goo, by our marriage, by the life we had shared. Now Hyung Goo was dead. I was not his wife; I was his widow. And yet, becoming a widow was not an event but a process. It took time to let go of that old, familiar, dying self, the self that had been Hyung Goo's wife, and time to greet the infant self, the self that was born the night that Hyung Goo died.

At first grief seemed solid, impenetrable, like a boulder that had landed on top of me. Did I dare to feel relief? Hyung Goo was no longer living with terminal illness. Neither was I. But to feel relieved would require acknowledging how hard it had all been, not only for Hyung Goo but also for me. I wanted to believe that it had been a good decision to marry one another; that we had had a full and happy life together. If I really thought seriously about everything that had happened, would I still think it had been worth it in the end? Or would I conclude that it had all simply been too sad?

At the same time I wanted to do it all over again, only this time getting everything right: not worrying him needlessly, not demanding so much of him, not arguing with him. In a corner of my mind I knew that without these things we would have had less together, not more. I still felt like I hadn't done enough for him. Did I say the right things? Do the right things? Tell him I loved him enough? I wished I could have been God to him, and given him the desires of his heart. For the first time I began to understand the prayers of the Requiem Mass. Here were all the things I wished for Hyung Goo: rest and peace and light and, above all, joy.

I was tired all the time. As the months ticked by I got tireder and tireder. It seemed that I was tired deep down inside, not just physically but emotionally, not just from the strain of Hyung Goo's last few weeks and months of life but from years before that. I felt twice as tired as I had thought it was possible to be. I couldn't imagine being able to sleep enough not to be tired any more. I had always slept well. Hyung Goo had been an insomniac. After he died, I started to have all the sleep problems he used to have. I would wake up in the middle of the night, be unable to get back to sleep, and then get up late in the morning feeling more tired than I had when I had gone to bed the night before.

As Hyung Goo had become more ill, his appetite and sense of taste had been affected. The ordinary task of thinking of something to have for dinner had become a seemingly insurmountable obstacle, one that was encountered every single day: What would he be able to eat? What might appeal to him? Sometimes he would choke down a meal for which he had no appetite, only to throw it all up again, leaving both of us close to tears of exhaustion and frustration: here I had gone to the trouble of cooking, and he had gone to the trouble of eating, and it hadn't done any good and we had to start over. After Hyung Goo died, I dissolved in tears every time I sat down to eat. I couldn't or didn't want to eat anything that he and I had eaten. I could hardly stand to go to the grocery store. I subsisted on tuna fish and grilled cheese for months.

I felt utterly alone. Part of being married had been the joint-ness of the effort. Marriage could only be done together; it was always more than the sum of its parts. But widowhood could only be done alone. It seemed inescapably solitary. When Hyung Goo died, I thought, "That was the hardest thing I will ever do. Grieving for Hyung Goo cannot possibly be harder than what I have already done." I was right. Grief was not as bad, or at least it wasn't any worse. But I had done Hyung Goo's death together with him. Grief I had to do alone. This was surely the hardest thing I had ever tried to do without him. I had only learned to be a human being together with Hyung Goo. How could I possibly grieve for him by myself?

In fact, I did not grieve for Hyung Goo by myself. For all my feelings of existential isolation, grief was intrinsically, inescap-ably social. I went for walks or had dinner with friends who had been present near the center or around the edges of our life in Durham. I spent hours on the telephone. I traveled all over the country, from New England to California, from New Orleans to Chicago, visiting my relatives and his relatives, my friends, his friends, our friends. Everywhere the agenda was the same: to talk about Hyung Goo and about our life together, to listen to others' memories of him and of us, and thus together to survey the ground upon which my new life and self and relationships would eventually be built.

As I told the stories over and over again, the seeming solid-ity of grief began slowly to waver and dissolve. It was not the same all the way through; it was complex and multiform. It wasn't just one thing; it was many things. I began to see them looming up before me, like mountain peaks in the mist: issues to be explored and thought through and dealt with, too many to do all at once, each too big to do all at one time. They seemed to cluster into two questions: What had I lost? Who had I become?

I mourned for the children we had never had. I had felt the loss of our children strongly in the first couple of years we were married, but had done so less as Hyung Goo became sick and our attention was consumed in coping with his illness. Now that old grief began to move back from the periphery to nearer the center. Perhaps I might still have children. It didn't seem likely, but it was imaginable. It was certain that I would never have Hyung Goo's children. I would never meet them, never know their quirks and personalities, never see them smile or hear them laugh or take them to the library or to the zoo. I would never grow old seeing him in them.

I mourned for the Hyung Goo I had never known. The Hyung Goo I really knew, after we had been married awhile, was always sick. I could hardly remember a time when he hadn't been ill. As I sorted through his things, I found boxes of sports equipment: hockey skates, a basketball, a softball glove. I had never seen him play hockey or basketball or softball. I found old photographs from hiking trips he had made in the White Mountains. We had never gone hiking together. I found his conductor's baton, annotated scores, old compositions. Hyung Goo had never begun to fulfill his potential as a musician. He had suffered too many wounds ever to have been able to pour himself into music or anything else as he might have done in a different, better world.

I mourned for who we might have been, had we had more time. Had it really been only four years since we had been married? "Four years isn't long," a friend said to me, "but it seems that you packed at least twenty years of living into that four years." Somehow, that seemed right. I knew it wasn't like fifty years, but it seemed like twenty. A person who is twenty years old is just arrived on the brink of adulthood—not mature adulthood, but adulthood. She has weathered most of the storms of adolescence; she is not a child anymore. She is poised just on the brink of something new, of all kinds of possibilities—and it was just at this point that our shared life had ended, and with it all the possibilities, all the might-have-beens, that were inherent in it.

I mourned for our public persona as a couple. An elderly lady, offering condolences, said to me, "You two were so close. You had something that many people never have." Her words echoed comments made by many others during our marriage. People seemed to be able to see, just by looking at us, the deeply intimate connection we had forged with one another. With Hyung Goo gone, that sense of public presence was gone too. New acquaintances met only me, not him or us. How could this be? I was myself only in and with him. It couldn't possibly be me they were meeting, not really. It was only a shadowy, empty sort of me. I felt I had lost not only Hyung Goo, but myself as well.

I was startled to realize that my new, widowed self was not a pure negation. There was someone there, someone I hardly recognized. I seemed to be emerging from my years with Hyung Goo a very different person from the one I had been when I married him. I had never been sure of myself or of anyone else. Hyung Goo and I had learned to trust each other. When he died, he left me a legacy of confidence: a confidence that I could manage, and that I would find the help I needed. I had lived in a fog of barely-acknowledged sorrow. Together, Hyung Goo and I had found joy. When he died, he left me a remembered happiness that seemed mysteriously to extend even into the grief of losing him. I had longed for love but feared I would never find it. Hyung Goo had loved me with every particle of himself. When he died, he left me a peace rooted in that love.

Everywhere I looked in my life, there were people. They all seemed to be telling me the stories of their lives, and wanting to hear the story of mine. When had I become a person whose life was so intertwined with those of so many others? My life seemed to be taking shape as if it were a tree, with Hyung Goo and me together forming the trunk, and all of my subsequent relationships and connections forming the branches, all far richer and more complex than I had ever imagined possible. It was an image at once powerful and upsetting. I wanted Hyung

Goo, not a beautiful life without him. I wanted time to stop. I didn't want anything ever to change. I wanted to be miserable forever, lest in any subsequent happiness I forget the primal happiness we had experienced together.

Of course change came. It came immediately, unbidden and unwelcome. I was surprised by a rainy day. Hyung Goo had watched the weather daily; I hadn't seen a forecast in weeks. I stopped to get gas and thought to check the oil. I had to hunt for the dipstick. Hyung Goo had always checked the oil; I never had. I did laundry, wondering why there were so few clothes. Then I realized: I was doing wash for only one person. While Hyung Goo had been alive, I had loved him more every day. I didn't see how I could continue to do that now that he was dead. And what I wanted least of all was to love him less, miss him less, think of him less.

I suspected then what it took months and even years fully to appreciate: that there would one day come a time when change would not spell decay. There would come a time when missing Hyung Goo differently would not mean missing him less. There would come a time when I would miss not happiness in general, as if I couldn't be happy without him, but the particular happiness we had found together. I would miss Hyung Goo for who he was and for who we were together. I would appreciate our marriage not as the perfect pattern by which all other marriages were to be judged, but as having been uniquely right for us, uniquely precious because it was ours, but hardly the only way to be married. Other people, other lives, other marriages might be completely different and yet equally precious.

One day I would recognize the kaleidoscopic quality of grief. The kaleidoscope cannot not turn; it is as inexorable as the tide. Early on the patterns are bold and the colors bright and deep. With the passage of time the patterns and colors become more muted. Memories shift and change; perceptions of the past alter with subsequent experience. And yet, that past remains what it was. None of its pieces are lost; rather, they tumble against one another, forming new patterns, receiving and transmitting light in sometimes familiar, sometimes startling, ways.

Some years after Hyung Goo's death I was asked, along with several other women, to describe an occasion on which body, soul and spirit had formed a "holy trinity" of sorts. One woman told a story about being pregnant; another described an experience of childbirth. As I listened to them speak, it occurred to me that being with Hyung Goo when he died was as close as I had ever come to giving birth—the intensity and pain and focus had been so all-consuming, and through it both Hyung Goo and I had been birthed into new lives. As I told the story of the last days and hours of his life, the emotions I had felt at the time came rushing back, overwhelming and engulfing me. I was struggling to speak through tears; when I finished, all I could hear was everyone else crying.

The experience left me deeply shaken. I was utterly exhausted, and, as I was no longer used to coming completely unglued in public, I felt a little foolish besides. And yet, it was an oddly reassuring experience as well. A shaft of light had glinted through the kaleidoscope, and I had been reminded how integral a part of me my life with Hyung Goo, and my sorrow over his death, still were. I no longer felt my grief for him with that intensity every day, but it was still there. It was permanently a part of me, even as Hyung Goo himself had been permanently woven into the fabric of my very self.

# MAY 13, 1996: FINAL EXAM

There had always been a degree of risk to my health as long as I was married to Hyung Goo. It was this, more than anything else, that mystified my friends and acquaintances as they thought about my decision to marry Hyung Goo. A lot of them seemed to view that decision as utterly without parallel, completely unlike any decision that they could ever make or could imagine anyone making. Didn't I realize that AIDS was an infectious disease? What if I caught it from him? How could I possibly expose myself to such a risk?

These thoughts had occurred to us. Before we were married, we took a good hard look at the epidemiology of AIDS, and decided that, with certain precautions, we could be reasonably confident I wouldn't be infected. We would use a condom every single time we had sex. We would make sure I didn't come in contact with blood on needles or dressings or everyday cuts and scrapes. These measures wouldn't eliminate all risk of transmission, but they would reduce it to a level both of us were willing to live with. And beyond this, we tried not to think about it. We had made our decision. We were doing everything we thought appropriate in the way of minimizing risk to my health, and we couldn't dwell morbidly on awful possibilities and still have energy for living out our life together.

But a minimal risk is still a risk. We knew there was always a possibility that I could become infected, and so every six or eight months, I would get an HIV test. I was not enthusiastic about this. I thought that I would be better off not knowing; that I could live better with a small degree of uncertainty than

213

I could with the unlikely reality of a positive test. I wondered whether Hyung Goo himself might have been better off not to have known when he did. But Hyung Goo thought I should be tested, his physicians advised it, and it did seem reasonable. So every so often, I would go to the health department and get another test.

I had my HIV tests at the Durham County health department, because this was the only place where anonymous HIV testing was available. If you went anywhere else, the most secure option was so-called confidential testing, in which, if you tested positive, your name was sent to the state and entered in a computer database. This didn't strike me as particularly confidential. Bad enough to test HIV-positive; far worse to have your HIV status on file with the state, where anyone with enough determination and bad will could get into that database and prevent you from getting health insurance, life insurance, even housing or employment, ever again.

So I went to the health department. In the waiting room, tired-looking people slumped in rows of plastic chairs while safe-sex messages, mostly involving actors dressed up like giant condoms, blared nonstop from the video machine. Ill-supervised, dirty children played on the floor while their parents waited to see the HIV counselors. The counselors appeared to believe that anyone who came in for an anonymous HIV test must be busy copulating with all and sundry, whatever they might say to the contrary. On hearing that I had had sex only with my husband, and never "unsafely," they would respond with astonishment, if not visible skepticism. "Well, try to keep the numbers down," one of them said to me.

I would come away from these encounters feeling repelled and disoriented. What was I doing here in this place with these people? I wanted to pin a sign to myself saying, "Married. Chaste. Better than you." Did these people have any idea what kind of sexual behavior is truly human? What had happened to the world to make chastity look so weirdly aberrant? And yet, for all my sense that the health department was alien territory, I did belong there. Those people were at risk for HIV, and so was I.

214

After a while, we decided that the tests were more trouble than they were worth. They made both of us anxious, and the results made no practical difference to us. If a test was negative, all that told us was that what we were doing—or not doing—had worked so far. If it was positive, it was too late to do anything differently. I stopped getting tested. I decided that after Hyung Goo died, I would wait six months—the maximum time between initial infection and the appearance of antibodies that could be detected by standard HIV testing procedures—and then be tested one last time.

As the time approached, I began to wonder. What would it be like to know for sure I hadn't been infected? Being at risk for HIV had always been a part of life with Hyung Goo. We did our best to minimize the risk, but it was always there. But if my final test result was negative, I wouldn't be at risk any more. That part of the story would be over, even as so many other parts of the story were already over. I would know that I got out alive. I would know that we succeeded in what we set out to do—to preserve my health. And I would take yet another step away from the way things were when Hyung Goo was alive. We had lived together in the world of AIDS and HIV. Since his death, I had lived in that world alone. Would I now leave that place behind?

I went to the health department on April 30 and had my blood drawn. They gave me a slip of paper with a number on it, and told me to come back in two weeks. Hyung Goo and I had always gone together to retrieve my results. Now, in his absence, I asked Ruth, a friend from church, to go with me. We made a date for May 14. By May 13, one day shy of the two weeks, I was already feeling very queasy. I had an appointment with Dan that afternoon, and would certainly have spent at least part of that hour talking with him about the next day's pilgrimage to the health department. Then Dan called; he was sick, and would have to cancel our appointment. Now what would I do? I called Martha. Her opinion, after listening to my tale of woe, was that I just needed to get the test results and get it over with. I gave her my identifying number, and she called the health department. We knew they wouldn't give out results over the phone, but perhaps they would be willing to tell her whether the results were available. Yes, they were. She called me back, and told me to go on in, and to call her when I got back. I called Ruth, but she wasn't home. Unwilling to prolong the suspense any longer, I got in the car and went to the health department alone.

I was in and out in ten minutes. The HIV counselor took my slip of paper, left the room, and came back with the result. "Good news," she said. "It's negative." Her words landed like a spark on years of pent-up anxiety and grief. What had happened to Hyung Goo had been so awful. Would it happen to me, too? I started to cry, and then to shake. I wondered later what it would have been like to let the fire burn until it went out. But I really didn't want to sit there and cry alone in the presence of a total stranger. I pulled myself together, went home, and called Martha. Did I want to come in to the clinic and talk with her? Yes, I did.

I expected to be able to find my way back to those tears that I had clamped off at the health department, but I never did, not with Martha that afternoon, or with Dan later in the week, or ever. But it was comforting to talk to Martha, nonetheless. I hadn't done the therapeutic thing with her for a long time. It had felt good to feel her swing into action on my behalf, and it felt good to go into her office and hand all my mixed and tumultuous emotions off to her. Martha wondered whether survivor guilt was any part of what I felt. She saw a lot of this in HIV-negative partners of people with HIV. But survivor guilt, if I felt any, would surely have shown up earlier in things like risky behavior, which I never engaged in. No, I didn't feel guilty. What I felt was one more loss of connection to the past, to the way things used to be, to life with Hyung Goo. There were a lot of things about that life that neither one of us liked, and my being at risk for HIV was near the top of the list; but it had been a shared and much-loved life, and I grieved for the way it was all vanishing, the good and the bad alike, into the past.

What would I have done if the test had come back positive? I don't know. I'm glad I never had to find out. But I wonder now how different my experience of risk for HIV was from the risks that so many others encounter in the course of their lives. I have friends who run a mission school in western Uganda. The guerilla fighting that spills over the Congolese border, into their district has displaced tens of thousands of people who crowd into filthy, disease-ridden refugee camps. My friends do their best to minimize the risks to themselves and their two young children. They take anti-malarial medication; they boil their water; they leave the area when the gunfire becomes too intense. But they always go back. Why? Why would anyone choose to live in a war zone? Possibly because she or he loves someone who can't live anywhere else. My friends love the children of Uganda. I loved Hyung Goo. He had no choice but to live with HIV and AIDS. How could I have lived anywhere else while he was there?

# DESCENDING

For months I lived in a kind of no-man's-land atop the mountain that Hyung Goo and I had spent our married life climbing. My options seemed completely open. I could go anywhere; I could do anything. No longer bound by the constraints that Hyung Goo's illness had imposed upon us, no longer focused by the very limits of that life, I felt at once free and lost. I was unsure what to choose, unsure that I wanted to choose anything. Everyone I knew always seemed to have plans, big plans. I never had any plans. I just wanted to sleep, or cry, or something.

And then one day I realized that I was no longer on that mountaintop. The feeling of being "done," of having finished my life's work, that had so encompassed me in the weeks and months following Hyung Goo's death, had shifted both subtly and definitively to a new sense of being "done with that." I was at the end of something, but no longer only at the end. I was at the beginning of something new. Without noticing the moment at which I had begun to descend, I had already come down through layers of cloud and was emerging into a space that was not yet fully in focus, but that I could tell was spacious and light and full of brighter colors than I had seen in a long while.

I left my journal on the mountaintop. It had served its purpose, as a kind of cistern to hold the floodwaters of emotion in the first year or so after Hyung Goo died. But the soil in the foothills was fertile, moist, well-drained. I was no longer continually flooded by my experiences, whether of happiness or of sorrow. They soaked into my life and self like rain soaks into the ground, not directly accessible but not lost either, ready to nurture whatever is planted there.

# LIVING ON THE OCEAN

Several years after Hyung Goo died, I spent an afternoon talking with a friend about Hyung Goo and about our marriage. The friend was a medical professional, and asked a number of specific questions about the medical side of the story. As a result, I found myself working hard to remember a lot of details that I hadn't had much reason to think about for a long time.

That night I dreamt I was talking to a woman at a hotel reception desk. The receptionist asked me about my name, and I told her that the "Kim" in my name was not an American first name, but a Korean last name. I had been married to a Korean, I explained, and Kim was his family name. I took his name as mine, and when some years after his death I remarried, I kept the "Kim" as part of my name. This seemed to strike the person in my dream as evidence of extravagant devotion. "You must still feel married to him," she said, earnestly. "No," I said, cheerfully. "I feel married to my present husband, but I still think of him very fondly."

This was a new dream. On a number of occasions after my remarriage, I had had dreams in which Hyung Goo reappeared, apparently not dead after all. In these dreams, my emotions ranged from nonplussed to consternated. I would think, "What do I do now? I've gone and married someone else, and now it turns out he's not dead. How could I have made such a mistake? He really did look dead. I think this is illegal." I took these dreams as evidence that, on some level, my psyche hadn't quite caught up with my life. Yes, I had remarried, but somewhere in me I didn't quite believe it. This dream seemed to say that now

I really did believe it, and it was just fine. I remembered Hyung Goo very fondly, and I was married to someone else now.

A year or so later I had another dream. I dreamt that I was standing with Hyung Goo's sister, Grace, in a bright, open space, which somehow we knew was the outskirts of heaven. We were talking with Hyung Goo; it seemed that he had been on his way to a rehearsal, and upon seeing us had come over to greet and speak with us. He was addressing Grace, asking her questions, conveying his delight in seeing her after what had been a long separation. He was radiant with joy, his face full of love and welcome and that simultaneously grave and lively interest that was so characteristic of him. As they talked, I stood off to the side, looking on, crying and crying and crying.

In the dream, it seemed obvious why I was crying: because I missed Hyung Goo so much. But why was it only I who was crying? Did Hyung Goo somehow miss me less, love me less, than I missed and loved him? I don't know whether I wondered this in my dream, or whether I wondered only afterward as I woke from my dream in the middle of the night, still feeling myself shaking with sobs. But the answer seemed clear enough: Hyung Goo is dead, and precisely because he is dead, he can love without grief. Is this not what it means to stand in the presence of God—to have one's every tear be wiped away, leaving only joy? The medievals called such a person a *comprehensor,* one who knows as he is known, one who loves as God loves, without any admixture of sorrow. But I am still a *viator,* a pilgrim, one who can love only in the midst of loss; and when confronted, in my dream, with the one with whom I had shared so great a love, I could do nothing but cry.

Which of these dreams is my life now? They both are. It is like living in a little house on the shore of a new country full of interesting and beautiful things just waiting to be discovered and explored. The front door of the house faces inland, toward roads and hills and mountain vistas. Out the back door is the beach, and beyond it, an ocean of tears, on the far side of which is a land that used to be home but that is so no longer. When the wind is off the land, the weather is sunny and dry and clear. When the wind is off the ocean, the mists and fog roll in. And always, in rain and sun alike, there is the gentle lapping of the tide against the shore.

221

# ACKNOWLEDGEMENTS

This book constitutes an extended note of thanks to all of the people named or alluded to in its pages. Their presence during my time with Hyung Goo and afterwards has immeasurably enriched my life.

Thanks are due in addition to:

Hal and Betsy Piper, in the reception of whose hospitality it first occurred to me to wonder what I might say, if I were ever to try to offer an account of Hyung Goo's and my life together.

Daniel Gawthrop and Jane Griner, who wrote the song *Sing Me to Heaven*, and to Rodney Wynkoop, who introduced me to it.

Rodney Clapp, who offered me a contract, without which assuredly the book would never have been written.

The Alumnae Association of Mount Holyoke College, which supported the writing of the manuscript with an Alumnae Fellowship.

Betsy Morgan, colleague, friend, in-house editor and all-around encourager.

Dwight Peterson, to whom it is a pleasure to be married.

Mark Peterson, whose arrival made me both a mother and a writer.